Gardens, Covenants, Exiles

DENNIS DUFFY

Gardens, Covenants, Exiles:
Loyalism in the Literature of
Upper Canada/Ontario

UNIVERSITY OF TORONTO PRESS
Toronto Buffalo London

© University of Toronto Press 1982
Toronto Buffalo London
Printed in Canada
ISBN 0-8020-5561-3 (cloth)
ISBN 0-8020-6477-9 (paper)

Canadian Cataloguing in Publication Data
Duffy, Dennis, 1938–
Gardens, covenants, exiles
Includes index.
ISBN 0-8020-5561-3 (cloth); ISBN 0-8020-6477-9 (paper)
1. United Empire Loyalists in literature.
2. Canadian literature (English) – Themes, motives.*
I. Title.
PS8103.U5D83   C810'.9'358   C81-094775-7
PR9185.6.U5D83

33,182

To my mother and to the memory of my father

Contents

Preface

The idea for this study came from two of its subjects, George Grant and Hugh Hood, whose writings first made me aware of the rootedness of the culture of Upper Canada. My intellectual debt to them can never be repaid.

Dennis Lee gave an earlier draft his thorough, generous, and exacting scrutiny. Although the result has not reached the heights he and I would wish, his free gift of his insight and intelligence has brought it a little closer to acceptability.

Carl Berger gave encouragement and advice to me, and further encouragement came from Michael Bliss, Germaine Warkentin, William Westfall, and Lynne Young. Naturally, none of these is responsible for any of this work's flaws.

A portion of a chapter of this book appeared originally in the *Journal of Canadian Studies*.

The staffs of the Trinity College Library, the Metropolitan Toronto Library, the Robarts Library, and the Thomas Fisher Rare Book Library of the University of Toronto have been helpful to my enterprise. I am also grateful to the typists – Emma Pohl, Cynthia Burton, Kathy McCallum, and especially Audrey Perry – who put up with a great deal, and cheerfully; thanks also to Trinity and Innis colleges in the University of Toronto, who provided me with these typists' services. My editors at the University of Toronto Press, Gerry Hallowell and Mary McDougall Maude, proved unable to transform brick into marble; they did, however, perform quite a bit of tuck pointing.

This book has been published with the help of grants from the Canadian Federation for the Humanities, using funds provided by the Social Sciences and Humanities Research Council of Canada, and from the Publications Fund of University of Toronto Press.

Finally, my wife Mary Ann neither read nor commented on the work, but only gave me unfailing encouragement and optimism in times of doubt. And those are the sweetest gifts of all.

Gardens, Covenants, Exiles

Introduction

I

In this book, I attempt to describe and analyse the effects of United Empire Loyalism on the literary culture of what is now Ontario. My task resembles that of relatives at the unveiling of the new-born: 'She has her father's ears.' 'No, that's her great-aunt's chin.' So many things go into our making. History remains an inexact science, the working of the imagination mysterious, and the link between the two an underground stream. Even that analogy breaks down, because I am trying to map that stream without the benefit of tracing dyes. Obviously, if the observer drops dye at point A and never finds it at B, then A–B are not points along an identical course. Facts never lie.

How can one then deal with an intuition about a culture? Merely locating resemblances cannot demonstrate identity. My thesis – the enduring nature of an attitude of mind whose historical origins lie in the Loyalist experience – is the dye. But the course that tincture runs is also of my making. The only 'legitimate' procedure for this undertaking would involve the consideration of specific references to United Empire Loyalism in our literature, imaginative and discursive. Such an enterprise would produce no more than what we know already – that the Loyalists founded this province, and that historians, novelists, and social commentators have at times overestimated or underestimated their contribution to Upper Canada/Ontario, and have at times rendered it due estimation. But where would that leave the things we do not know? What would happen to the whole grand process of hypothesis and speculation that keeps culture's shrine from decaying into a mausoleum?

Back to the baby: no relative will ever know for sure whether that chin came from the father or the delivery man. No determinist genetic code shapes the facts of history and culture. Yet how timid to balk at speculation, to funk the challenge to trace a theme through its many appearances within a culture!

What follows remains a hypothesis, an attempt to view a literature selectively and through what is at times a distorting glass. Without that hypothesis and even distortion, how can the features ever show themselves? My task involves showing an aspect of our culture that has struck no other critic so fully as it has me. This scarcely contends that I am right and everyone else wrong. It does assert that greater attention must be paid to the habit of mind I outline whenever anyone attempts to gain a full view of the culture of Upper Canada/Ontario. If this essay produces no more profound result than a critic's refutation of it, it will have served its purpose, that of heightening our sense of a culture's roots.

II

Scraps, tags, figments of the Loyalist heritage dot our landscape. The United Empire Loyalist Association meets annually, publishes a newsletter, and sponsors speakers and museums. The provincial crest enjoins us to remain as loyal as when we began. Highway plaques remind us of our origins, should we pause long enough to read them. One of Ontario's most beautiful roads, highway 33, winds along the lakeshore from Kingston to Trenton, before heading north to disappear at Stirling. Among the settlements it passes through stands Adolphustown, where the Loyalists first landed, and travellers on 33 take a ferry from there to the peninsular Prince Edward County.[1] One of those tiny arks is named *The Quinte Loyalist* and one wonders what the tourists – and the natives as well – make of it.

Something of Loyalism lies in our air, and in our very provincial life. Its explicit political and social consequences have been examined by various historians, yet no one has undertaken to consider its influence on our literary culture. Loyalism, both as myth and fact, has bequeathed to us a certain habit of mind expressing itself in our literature as well as in our political behaviour. Can one sense this presence without attempting to pass it off as some all-encompassing First Cause that has worked its way inexorably through our literary experience?

When Glendower declaims in *Henry IV Part I* that he can call spirits from the deep, he speaks as a surveyor of mythology. Hotspur's devastating reply – 'But will they come?' – does not deny the value of the enterprise, only his opponent's power to bring it off. In the Loyalist myth, I am seeking to call forth a symbolic pattern of explanation and narration laid upon the stark facts of defeat, exile, endurance, and final mastery of a new land. Out of a communal trauma of defeat, exile, and beginning again comes a larger patterning. The events are now viewed within a larger framework of endurance and final vindication through political and material success. The myth then assumes a cautionary stance: 'Beware, lest what has once passed through the wiliness and treachery of your enemies pass from you again through your own indifference and faint-heartedness.'

Students of literature who write about myth trust that their audience will not take the term as a synonym for 'lie.' But what happens once we cease using it to describe the cyclical narratives of the doings of gods and heroes? For example, we know that something happened to the way western man sought to order his relationship to the world in the years between 1783 and 1867. Whether we call that time the industrial revolution, the fall of agrarian man, or the age of improvement (as does Asa Briggs in his 1959 volume of that name), we know that the process described did not burst suddenly and discontinuously on the scene. A host of historical events – the invention of the steam engine, the acquisition by Britain of Far Eastern textile markets, the rise of the secular state, among a myriad of other things – paved the way for the process we attempt to sum up with our various labels. Even to use a phrase like 'the rise of the secular state' demonstrates how we define one question-begging label by a recourse to another. Yet we bestow this shape upon history to grant it the coherence our minds seek by their very nature. We impose a beginning-middle-and-end kind of narrative structure on events which, like the relationships caught briefly in novels, have no limits beyond those we arbitrarily assign. This resembles myth-making; we do not in fact lie, but we humanize the truth of undifferentiated chaos through our own rage for narrative order. Thus the writing of history books presents itself as a dialogue. Some writers through the force of their insight compel us to label certain events and processes. Others seek to unravel what has been knitted together, revealing the extent to which a process has been foreshadowed, made more complex, and even contradicted by hitherto unaccommodated but relevant events.

That labelling enterprise, in essence, is the sort of myth that explains our collective experience, allowing us to classify the human project according to the progression of the ages of the Father, Son, and Holy Ghost, or to group together a few decades under the heading, the enlightenment. But if this is one use of myth, we also realize that like an opera plot, a lower usage of the term parodies and even undermines the more illustrious goings-on upstairs. Here myth comes close to lie: the stab-in-the-back version of Germany's defeat in World War I, the concept of a historic mission requiring the imposition of white rule over alien territories, and so on. Any student of culture and history deludes himself in believing that the high road can be taken without recourse at times to the low. So it is with the material examined here. Thus in the Loyalist myth, the events of the American Revolution appear no longer as discrete happenings. Just as the enclosure of the common land in England becomes a milestone in discussing the industrial revolution, so military disasters fall into place as parts of larger wholes which mitigate and even transform the agony of the catastrophes themselves.

As that metamorphosis happens, so must we make a series of sidesteps to keep the myth upright. Thus a working myth of the Loyalist achievement has to skirt the tangle of political and personal factors that compelled a minority of King George's American supporters to leave the American colonies and settle elsewhere. Instead, a voluntarist and idealist motivation accounts for their arrival here. We are told of a group too devoted to the crown to live beneath the rule of those who had overturned it. This leaves out the sort of people as those who calculatingly bet, but on the wrong side, or who involved themselves in acts too bloody to be forgiven. It also ignores what common sense would see as the majority: those who – wishing only to be left in peace – found themselves shoved by circumstance into an allegiance they would rather have fudged.[2]

Suppose one assumes that in choosing to support the king, the Loyalists accepted in some way beforehand the dire fate awaiting them. Still, many of the occupants of Upper Canada in the years before 1812 were the land-hungry rather than the loyal. This weakens the claim that Loyalism and Loyalists alone provided the province's chief defence during the war of 1812. The military element, the sense of 1812 as a second Loyalist war, alters uniquely the shape of the Loyalist myth in Upper Canada and distinguishes it from the non-violent Maritime myth. To satisfy the demands of the myth of the Upper Canadian militia, the colonists' reliance upon the British regulars gets played down. To cap all this, a simplistic pattern of Loyalist fidelity vs Late Loyalist shiftiness, which the facts hardly bear out, comes to be the received version of the facts.[3]

This blurring of historical fact comes about not only through a community's desire to provide itself with elevating images, but out of the need to satisfy profound longings in the western mind. Images of exile in the wilderness followed by the occupation of Canaan, images of gardens regained: the strength and solace these offer make inevitable that the historical facts take a beating whenever they come up against such symbolic expressions.

To give the reader some sense of the power of the myth and manner in which it reshaped the rougher edges of history, let me turn to the autobiography of Steven Jarvis (1756–1840) as edited by his great-grandson,

Thomas Stinson Jarvis, and serialized in four issues of a popular journal in 1909.[4] The account presents an honest profile of a man confident in his acquisitiveness. Jarvis makes no bones about his ambitions for high rank in Simcoe's Rangers (166–7), his moral lapse in gambling away his unit's pay-chest (216–17), the prosperity that comes his way as a Fredericton shopkeeper (228–9), and his forceful pleas for a patronage job in the administration of Upper Canada after he moved here (247–8). When bankruptcy – the result of wartime overstocking – falls upon Jarvis, he first secures a government job and then repairs to his wealthy parents in the United States 'to embrace this opportunity to secure what I considered my due share in what my Father should die possessed of' (257–60). His descendant dresses up this single-minded, thoroughly pragmatic figure who could have sprung from the pages of Smollett and turns him into one of the touching fossils a reader might encounter in *Guy Mannering* or *Redgauntlet*:

If memory rightly serves, these bows [made as gentleman usher of the black rod in the legislative assembly] were made into empty space – to the supposed presence of a King, who, to him as well as to the other Loyalists, was an unseen ideal, the 'Fountain of Honour,' and the supposed personification of all the known virtues. He had been doing this always. Figments of the Imagination were his life's anchorages. To these he lived, loved, fought, and died, loyal. For Wife, children, friends, and King – a Loyalist. (266)

The narrative and the editor's comments display the myth in action, Jarvis' story is no aimless tale, but a picaresque novel on the order of *Tom Jones*. Here the hero arrives at his goal of a settled and dignified social position to replace the one he has lost for backing the losers in a civil conflict. His life acquires significance as an exemplar of 'Loyalism.' A career marked by an eye kept firmly on the main chance becomes an exemplum of idealistic commitment and impracticality. The temptation exists to write off this tacit dialogue between grabby ancestor and genteel descendant as a pack of lies. The workings of a culture, however, are never that simple. The above transaction plays a small part in a grand cultural enterprise. I seek to outline the shape taken by a particular cast of mind that grows not only out of historical experience but more important out of the reworkings of that experience.

Men must give shape to their lives, a shape that thrusts a possible future into their consciousness, a shape whose specific contours link it with past, hallowed forms of explanation. Satisfying those needs produced two achievements that this study examines: first, a wide substratum of cultural consensus upon which the individual writer could build his particular imaginative structure; secondly, a pattern of explanation which, even when unacknowledged or evoked indirectly, loomed behind the individual shapes taken by the primal myth.

III

What did this consensus assert? It held, essentially, that Canada in its perilous uniqueness remained a political and cultural entity whose preservation and enhancement signified the role that morality played in history. That Canada existed at all testified to the strength of the covenant between two parties, the colonials and the imperial power. The year 1812, according to the Loyalist myth, demonstrated that imperial citizens would not ignore the ties that had earlier granted them deliverance. They would place their property and persons in some jeopardy to preserve their new land from the menaces of the American republic, even when the motherland failed to supply them with sufficient soldiers (or military leaders bold enough) to thrust back the invader. The covenant stood. Its original manifestation had been the fidelity to the king's cause. That loyalty had earned them a place of refuge when their fidelity proved disastrous politically. Then had come the process of settlement and survival by which a one-time wilderness came to fruition in the hands of its stewards. The test of 1812 had bonded the contracting parties closer; the maintenance of the tie meant that any temporary trials and setbacks would be overcome through the renewed force of the original commitment.

The covenant made possible a land perched precariously between a wilderness on the one hand and an aggressive enemy on the other. What seemed a political and geographical impossiblity could be preserved only by adhering to the pact. Here stood a land and a degree of prosperity stemming not from conquest and enslavement, but from the toil of those who improved the empire that nurtured them. The empire not only nurtured them, it gave protection and an ideal of civil behaviour which set them apart from the oath-breakers to the south. Canada was perilous and unique because it depended upon mutuality, trust, and cohesion in the face of a continental power acknowleding no laws but its own, a power unable to play a proper role in the comity of states and powerless to impress upon its citizens proper standards of behaviour.

The literature produced by these convictions would display both inclusiveness and exclusivity. It would be the literature of the club, the tribe, the garrison. On the one hand stands a group of insiders needing to bury any mutual enmities of the past, seeking by compromise and reconciliation to arrive at a common front against envious outsiders; on the other dwell the outsiders and their insider allies. Thus the literature emphasizes the threat posed to solidarity by compelling, even heroic individuals who fail to keep in mind the larger communal purposes. Hence the delight taken in endurance and survival, viewed not as mere passive and inert states, but instead as proofs that the covenant still held. Fidelity and all it signified could still be said to hold its place within a troubled world. The ultimate implications of such a belief could be near chiliastic, though none of the writers pursued logic to such an extreme. Yet their sense of nationhood – however limited by their assumption that the experience of Upper Canada applied to all of Canada – possessed considerable resonance, based as it was on the sense of a land redeemed by the agency of a providential fall.[5] It shines forth from one of the earliest Loyalist statements: 'How mysterious are the ways of Providence! How shortsighted are we! Some years ago I thought it a great hardship to be banished into the wilderness and would have imagined myself completely happy could I have exchanged it for a place in the delightful city of Philadelphia. Now the best wish we can form for our friends is to have them removed to us.'[6]

The paradise lost, the war won in heaven by the wicked angels, is eclipsed by the paradise regained in the form of a new land to be built on surer foundations than the old. The passage from Good Friday to Easter showed that all things were possible for men who lived up to their obligations of fealty. Of course human nature, fallen nature, itself strove against this ideal, and therefore the works examined set forth fearful visions of disaster as well as affirmations of victory. Diversity and the double vision mark the literature, despite its striving to present a univocal and reassuring vision of the possibilities for Canadian endurance and achievement.

IV

You do not have to be a Loyalist ... Those ways of viewing Canada and its destiny were not peculiar to Loyalism alone. A rich British imperial and conservative tradition existed which offered considerable space to ideas of that sort. Yet this country, province, colony held a visible, well-defined, and historically rooted conduit through which that whole view of man and society could be funnelled. The historical process by which the Loyalists fled or were expelled and came to remember and celebrate that exodus gives to their vision an immediacy in Upper Canadian life. Here lay the roots of a conservative vision, a repugnance for rapid or violent social change and a deep attachment to the traditions of western civility. It was not a matter of ancient precedent and philosophical positions alone, but a view shaped by specific, recollected, ordered, and embellished historical events.

Nowhere does the essay seek to examine Loyalism and its ramifications as *the* cause of the conservative temper so marking Upper Canada's affairs and culture. Such reductionism would be at once simplistic and fallacious. Yet that tradition in all its literary ramifications needs examination because it remains the local colouring, the particular, regional ingredient to a broadly based western tradition. We are talking of a wave that has left its traces upon a shore. No observer can delineate all the contours of that past surge, though he can note that, yes, tones of this particular deposit exist elsewhere in the world. Yet we note that the substance also lives here. Common sense would assert that there is some relationship between the deposit and its source, though a precise analysis cannot be provided.

If the student accepts that that peculiar substance found in our literature has been ignored or forgotten, swept up into near-cosmic perspectives on Canadian cultural life in which lucid particularities disappear, then he must venture a risk. He must chance that his argument will be mistaken for an attempt at a single explanation or magic-key view of culture. The alternative is to let currents of thought and feeling continue to run submerged and largely ignored, and it is obvious which path I have chosen. The reader can best judge whether he has been alerted, or merely fooled.

Once the decision has been made to pursue a topic single-mindedly in the conviction that the reader can place this essay within his own context of the relative importance of cultural themes, a further problem arises. Someone opens a box of jewels. What is most interesting about the contents of the box? Is it the fact that they are all jewels, or the fact that each presents a different impression – both in itself and in its setting – from every other one? Surely there has to be a way to describe the objects themselves without losing sight of their common characteristics. Indeed there is, but in specific instances a reader – for I must leave my analogy now – may feel that he has been told more than he needs to know about a particular work or another and less than he wants to know about the general thesis that links these works and writers together. My own bias holds that nothing interests so much as particularity and specificity. Here I must again live with the risk that I have perpetrated a series of discrete essays rather than what I am attempting: a coherent essay retaining an amplitude sufficient to explore the particular. Once again, my conviction is of less moment than my reader's response.

The sections of the book vary with the sort of material they seek to analyse. The opening chapter, a survey of the origins and nature of Loyalism in Upper Canada, acquaints the reader with the traumatic and complex nature of the Loyalist experience itself. It also suggests the unspoken concerns that lie behind any attempt to deal imaginatively with the experience. The next chapter deals with William Kirby, and the third jumps backward chronologically to talk of the writings of Major John Richardson. An argumentative reason explains this: my aim is to present a vision of Loyalism fulfilled before examining a literature of fear. In Kirby, the building of Upper Canada bears the impress of a paradise regained; the history of Canada's second founding race appears as a product of loyalty and a patriotism rooted in its associations with a specific space. All the triumphs in Kirby are by implication denied in Richardson. It is his despairing insight into the brittle nature of social institutions that makes his writings – those *of* a Loyalist rather than writings directly *about* Loyalism – so necessary to consider in coming to any understanding of the kind of sensibility caught in these pages.

To Kirby and Richardson alike, 1837 proved a third Loyalist war. They sidetracked the issues of responsible government and rule by an oligarchy and reduced the entire conflict to a matter of loyalty.[7] For Charles Mair, 1812 remained the focal point of Canadian history, with Tecumseh, the militia, and Brock serving as rescuers of the threatened land. Mair's work carefully avoids its own tragic and ironic implications, though a study of it discloses the sense of a threatened enclave and the fragility of the enterprises man carries out in an effort to realize his hopes.

The chapters on Kirby, Richardson, and Mair are followed by a brief section discussing a single novel, Wilfred Campbell's *A beautiful rebel* (1909). Its diversities in tone, its problems in finding a single ground to speak from, its shifts and compromises in its attempts to create a unified (Upper) Canadian social vision sum up many of the difficulties outlined in the chapters preceding it.

Canada's best-known novelist, Mazo de la Roche, presents an expiring vision – loyal, stable, British – of the Upper Canada that the Loyalists sought to create and that the mythology claimed had actually been created. Jalna and its environs form the last imaginative dwelling place for the social vision at the heart of the Loyalism.

After Mazo, the deluge. A brief section discusses first, the shifts in the textbook and popular fiction treatment of Loyalism, illustrating how the myth was stripped of any moral relevance and left as a purely pragmatic endorsement of a work ethic. The chapter then examines how a contemporary novelist uses a work that, gently but firmly, relegates the historical fact to the status of a fossil. The final chapter deals with a number of contemporary writers. Some speak of the Loyalist heritage itself. Others incorporate into their appreciation of the state of Canada an image of exile and the kingdom that has been expressed in previous chapters. The journey thus returns to its starting point, in pain, loss, and the sense of a vanished home.

What I have written tries to articulate what I found abiding within a regional literature that was not mine by birth. The upshot of the study is a sense that in some way the culture of Upper Canada/Ontario remains continuous. It has kept faith with its origins. Ontario's ancestors remain buried but not dead beneath the steel-and-glass façade of the Province of Opportunity. Their message – of covenant, of fall, of paradise lost and regained and lost again – far from reassuring, far from digestible to many, continues to be spoken, even to the unhearing. That kind of speaking to the deaf, as Isaiah and Matthew alike attest, has been with western culture for quite a while.† In our own local way, it is with us still, here, now. Something of this book is about that.

---

† And he said, Go, and tell this people, Hear ye indeed, but understand not; and see ye indeed, but perceive not. Make the heart of this people fat, and make their ears heavy, and shut their eyes; lest they see with their eyes, and hear with their ears, and understand with their heart, and convert, and be healed. Isaiah 6: 9–10.

Therefore speak I to them in parables: because they seeing see not; and hearing they hear not, neither do they understand. Matthew 13:13.

1 The Experience

I

Upper Canada was generated by the same imperial spasm that had, however involuntarily, produced the United States. The United Empire Loyalists lost a war that grew out of one they had helped win.

A French statesman predicted that the British conquest of Canada would eventually separate the thirteen colonies from the empire. The hit-and-run frontier warfare perfected by the Canadians of New France and their Indian allies necessitated imperial protection for the British colonies. That menace removed, the expenses for that protection – and the restrictions on expansionism that were part of the empire's price for shelter – proved onerous. Less than fifteen years after a victory that gave them most of North America, the British were well on their way to losing the richest and most populous portions of this continent.

If what remained of British North America after the Revolution was to be held for the empire, then an expansion of Canada was in order. Territorial expansion was needed to counter the westward push of the former British colonies, which even during the war had captured forts along the Wabash as well as those of Lake Champlain, and a new kind of Canadian was required as well. The need was for unswerving loyalty. The war had seen the Yankee merchants of Montreal – the predator class for whom Canada had been conquered – attempt to join their brothers to the south, and only the resolution of a strong military governor had throttled the movement at birth. [1] In Nova Scotia, loyalty had been a matter of office-holding: the military/civil establishment at that imperial outpost had rallied behind their livelihoods. The hinterland small farmers and traders, however, had prayed for nothing so much as to be left alone and would have joined with gratitude any decisive winner.[2]

The refugees from the Revolutionary war were at once ineffaceably North American – their London exile convinced them they were no longer English, a feeling their hosts heartily reciprocated – and firm in their antipathy to a republican South.[3] The imperial government was to prove generous in its settlement of Loyalist claims. They were, for example, to do better by them than twentieth-century France for its colonial *émigrés*. But Benjamin West's allegorical canvas of a bountiful Britannia sheltering nearly everybody who could be squeezed in, overlooked the fact that the Loyalists willingly served in defeat the aims of an empire whose previous support had cost them so much.[4] Loyalist regiments had even helped to defend Jamaica against the French, a fact no less astonishing to the non-imperial mind than Canadians defending Flanders against the Germans in 1914–18.[5] A grand political symbiosis had attached the Loyalists and their patrons; mutual interests brought about an imperial redeployment shifting them from a battlefield they had lost to a fortress they would defend.

II

What had been that battlefield experience? Prince Fabrizio's Waterloo – that pit of confusion and theatrics whose shape no participant knew – resembles the Loyalists' war.[6] The time and place of the conflict were not of their choosing. From the beginning of the agitation, they had sought to remain aloof from the conflict. They attempted no purges of colonial legislative assemblies where strange and seditious doctrines were preached, destroyed no printing presses screaming of royal conspiracies against colonial freedoms and the right of all men to choose their own governors. When a clergyman who supported the right of the king in parliament to rule decked his pulpit with loaded pistols to insure his safety, when the leading citizens of Massachusetts had their property ravaged by mobs, when British soldiers, awkward and terrified in their role as Boston's police, were threatened, goaded, and successfully assaulted in an effort to make them discharge their muskets at their tormentors, when officers of the imperial government were flogged and tortured for carrying out their duties, the supporters of the crown had lamented the times and the customs.[7] They formed no counter-demonstration to the politicized funereal pomps of the dead in the 'Boston massacre,' lynched no prominent members of the mob, got up no assassination teams against their enemies. Instead, they replied rationally or satirically to the pamphleteers, made mild witticisms in the face of terrorists (the Reverend Mather Byles of Boston remarked that he would rather 'be ruled by one tyrant three thousand miles away, [than] by three thousand tyrants [not] a mile away'[8]), beseeched the authorities for more protection, but bridled at any roughness on the part of the soldiers. Finally, they found themselves forced to flee their properties and homeland in the face of an embittered, angry, and implacable enemy who had frustrated them at every turn.

Between this passivity and final flight had lain combat, but the overall pattern of Loyalist resistance had about it the air of doomed sleep-walking rather than of tragic resistance or brutal counter-revolution.[9] The inertia of the comfortable can be formidable; so can their bloodthirstiness once they perceive that their interests have been truly threatened. This kind of savage repression the Loyalists were unable to carry out. Surely a major cause of their quietude lay in the fact that Loyalism cut across class lines. Civil conflicts produce myths of Cavalier versus Roundhead. Depending on one's side, the losers can be characterized as traditional or hidebound, spontaneous or reckless, comfort-loving or gross, cultured or decadent. Myths tend to overlook the social groups they cannot absorb. For example, any popular mythology of the War Between the States has to overlook the fact that poor-white farmers in East Tennessee fought for the Union, while their Alabaman counterparts supported the Confederacy. Any accurate version of the activities of poor whites must include those divergent facts that destroy any myth of poor-white solidarity. In the same way, one cannot succumb to a vision of typical Loyalist ladies in ball gowns pacing the barren shores of Nova Scotia. Most Loyalist ladies, like their men, occupied ordinary social rank. Yes, the Loyalists had a share of the comfortable, the established. The bias of office-holders and Anglican clergy lay often (though far from always) toward the powers that were, but great landowners and merchants showed no such drift. Among what we would now term ethnic groups, the Highland Scots remained the most eager to serve the crown (a result of what they had learned after Culloden about the way the crown dealt with its enemies), but no array of facts has yet supported a profile of the American Tory that limits him to a particular social class or group.[10] The broad truth of this statement bears two consequences. First, Loyalists and rebels went about in civilian dress: no great disparities of occupation or social station made them easily identifiable to each other. Secondly, even the most hardened materialist must conclude that ideology played a major role in the making of an American rebel. Removal of the French empire's Canadian threat might have enabled the American colonists to conceive of separation from the crown and its defending armies as a real possibility. That material fact could well have assisted the spread of an anti-imperial ideology which held that the governed have the right to choose and depose their governors according to the canons of self-interest. Yet that conviction, which implied an inevitable collision with a strong monarchy, swept not only through interested groups who stood to gain directly from home rule, but caught up the less-involved as well. Rebellion's path did not resemble the skip and jump of the tornado, but the rising and widespread disturbance of the cyclone.

Of course, those individuals who found themselves shifted from their position of Royalist sympathizers to the roles of Tories, combatants, and Loyalist exiles viewed themselves as moderates. Some spotted as clearly as any Whig the need for greater colonial freedom within a reconstituted empire.[11] After all, they were not divided from the Whigs, at least initially, by vast differences in style and station. They, like their opponents, *believed*. They sided with the rulers of the freest social and economic system the world then offered. They knew that the greatest military power in the world could bring its powers to bear quickly and effectively upon any group of malcontents seeking to overthrow it. Why should the players have to provide to their kibitzers a justification of the game? Why elaborately define self-evident truths? Why should those who want only peace, order, and good government have to struggle as heartily to preserve it as the seditious trying to wreck it? Their opponents answered these questions that conservatives always ask during social upheaval by defying the king, forming alternative institutions, and mounting armed insurrection.

Assume that the men holding the ideas found in the Declaration of Independence first appeared as cloven-hoofed, potent, and avowed foes of all right-thinking men: still, the ideas themselves had not previously been assembled as a coherent social philosophy. A host of doctrines, traditions, and suppositions went into the ideological foundations of the American Revolution, from Whiggish versions of the Roman republic to Puritan demolitions of an Anglican monarchy.[12] A great many English-speaking persons believed in one or two of them. It was the new arrangement, the linkage of previously separate ideas, that came as a shock. There were Loyalist thinkers and Anglican divines (who had learnt of the unstoppable drift of radical movements during the English Civil War) who shrewdly sensed the direction of things, but the majority of those who would later find themselves in a civil war chose not to pursue their thoughts that relentlessly. Governors as astute as Thomas Hutchinson saw where things were headed, yet neither the imperial authorities nor his own supporters proved of much aid to him by the time things had arrived. His prescience about the separatist thrust of American Whiggism and his willingness to employ the resources of government against it had only got him branded as a conspirator against the rights of free-born Englishmen.[13]

Unreadied by either political involvement or logical acuity, aghast at the collapse of institutions they had not even felt needed much defending, the crown's supporters now found themselves forced to choose sides against their neighbours. What lay beyond acquiescence? Why, serving a military establishment no less alien to them than to their fellow Americans who were fighting pitched battles with it. That battlefield, already swept with confused alarms of struggle and flight, grew more chaotic as the nature of the war revealed itself.

III

The British army troubled the Loyalists nearly as much as it did the rebels. The distinction between Americans who supported the king and Americans who fought against him proved too subtle for the soldiers, especially when in pursuit of booty.[14] Professional troops tend to distrust civilians, especially those not readily distinguishable from the enemy. They despise the civilian-turned-soldier, especially when such amateurs are English civilians with an inbred mistrust of professional soldiers. As metropolitans, they also despise colonials, especially those they suspect of greater intellectual attainments. Finally, since the British army was one long process of envy flowing in one direction and contempt in another, a force crammed with nice distinctions of *ton* and seniority among near-identical fighting units, its members especially despised colonials-turned-soldiers who presumed to advise on the ready and easy way of reconquering their own country.

The Loyalist regiments — there were many, since some nineteen thousand loyal Americans were to bear arms for the crown – bore resounding titles (DeLancey's Brigade, the Prince of Wales' American Regiment, the King's Own Dragoons, the Queen's Rangers) as well as arduous military tasks, but the sort of warfare those bodies found themselves engaged in was a savage one of raid and counter-raid.[15] Westchester County in New York, for example, could have been magically transported to the ancient Scottish Highlands or to the *bled* of twentieth-century Algeria without any incongruities arising. It became an arena for cattle raiders, looters, and bloodthirsty avengers on both sides.[16] The border between the solidly loyal New York City and the teemingly rebellious upstate, it allowed neither side to establish unshakeable control. The willingness of both sides there to harry and burn their opponents gives an index to the savagery of the combat in disputed areas everywhere. Decades after the Revolution, in 1821, a great American romancer used that violent setting for his tale of wartime conflict and derring-do. James

Fenimore Cooper's *The Spy* indicates how much 'adventure' material that setting furnished. Most areas were not disputed. Those places which the army occupied openly displayed Loyalist leanings; in unoccupied areas rebel committees repeatedly seized the initiative. There they swiftly terrorized or drove out any opposition, even potential opposition, and ruled as a new government. Most people of Loyalist disposition did not fight for the crown, nor did most of their rebel counterparts fight for the Congress. But a healthy number of those who did fight for the crown did so because they had been given no option of neutrality. Where they controlled the scene, Continental watch committees exacted at least passive support for the war effort. A Loyalist who could not trim his sails to that wind – let alone to that of taking up arms against his king – either fled or was harried to the nearest army-occupied region and enrolled there in one of the provincial units. Thus he became a soldier with a grievance, one whose life had been disrupted, even impoverished, by enemy activity.

The war experience was not primarily one of pitched battle along the professional lines of eighteenth-century military standards. Those robust enough to take up arms witnessed savageries and skirmishes followed by vendettas, crop burnings and cattle raidings, midnight beatings, and confinement to fever-ridden swamps and underground prisons as loathsome as the abandoned copper mines of Simsbury, Connecticut. Those who marched beneath the king's colours had generally been through some version – *mutatis mutandis* – of the above. To endure defeat in this kind of immediate, personalized war was to suffer galling humiliation.

Nowhere was this more apparent than in the South. The year 1777 and the catastrophe at Saratoga compelled the imperial strategists to find a new scheme for prosecuting the conflict. Hindsight reveals that the bare facts of logistics in an age of sail and unrationalized bureaucracy made victory impossible under any circumstances. To the imperial strategists, the war seemed winnable. They thought it the activity of a fanatical minority which after the defeat of its military arm could be subdued eventually by a loyal and peace-loving majority.[17] (We know now that this always marks imperial thinking about colonial wars from Ireland to Vietnam.) The British planned their strategy accordingly. The region north of New York and its harbour was to be left alone, with Canada adequately defended against its thrusts. A mobile regular force would successively occupy the populous regions of the South, raising and organizing the troops of Loyalists who would come flocking to the royal standard. Once the Loyalist restorations had been set firmly in power, the army would move on to pacify new territories until New England and the hinterlands of the middle states were left a disaffected and impoverished rump. The final upshot of this strategy was Yorktown, but before that a region never marked by a fanatical devotion to the principles of non-violence became a scene of savage revolution and counter-revolution. While the Loyalists were never quite able to become an effective White Guard, the rebels as Red Guard grabbed back their territories as soon as the army passed on and avenged a dozenfold whatever cruelties the Loyalist regimes had perpetrated. Colonel Banastre Tarleton, a dashing, aristocratic war criminal out of Byron, may have slain his thousands at the Waxhaws, but Daniel Morgan slew his tens of thousands at the Cowpens. No wonder that John Graves Simcoe, later to be governor of Upper Canada, feared for the safety of his Loyalist unit at the Yorktown surrender, and urged his commander to ship the Queen's Rangers out before the surrender took effect.[18]

The post-Saratoga southern strategy revealed that the war could be won neither with the Loyalists nor without them. Their supposedly great and resolute numbers had been the foundation for any credible plan for victory. Yet they had not – and given the vigour of the rebels they probably could not have – appeared in the strength necessary to hold the territory initially occupied by the army. As soldiers in military formations, fighting alongside the imperial professionals, the Loyalists had shown they could hold their own with any opponent. But as civilian soldiers, as bands of outraged neighbours who could give as good as they got, and as White Guardsmen, who could smother republican terror with an effective counter-terror of their own, they had shown themselves as failures.[19] This may well have revealed a nobler moral stance, a keener sense of humanity, an endearing naïveté about the rules of political violence, but it also made them losers. One suspects that it is this fact, rather than any guilt over their mistreatment, that has made the Loyalists until recently of relatively slight interest to a nation of compulsive winners.[20]

IV

This then was the collective, searing experience the Loyalists brought to the new land. Along with disaster and defeat came the certainty that they had been unjustly and cruelly treated. Unable to quell the rising tide of dissent at a point short of rebellion, they had gone on to defeat in war and reprisal by the victors. Even though the great majority of Tory sympathizers had accepted the new regime and remained in the country after the war had been lost, the conflict had still sparked a rate of emigration far greater than that produced by the French Revolution.[21] Victory had not softened the winning side. The victors viewed their one-time opponents as reprobates and traitors to a self-evidently just and noble cause. Even the finest spirits among the victors, such as General Washington, sought nothing for the Loyalists but dispossession and dismissal. Those who had served the crown were to be purged from the holy shores, though not before they had been spoiled of every possession their opponents could grab. In the face of such hard-heartedness, the compensation offered by the imperial authorities (who had, after all, enlisted the men to fight in their campaigns) appeared as sweet and generous as the oil that had flowed down the beard, the beard of Aaron. The Loyalists came to view the crown as their only hope for something approaching justice in so brutal a world. A band apart within the empire, they and their descendants would be granted the privilege of placing the letters 'UEL' (United Empire Loyalist) after their names. Sir Guy Carleton's refusal to conclude the occupation of New York until all Loyalists who sought deliverance had made their way to his ships must have appeared to them as the deeds of a latter-day Noah, preserving a saving remnant from a universal deluge.

Arriving first at Nova Scotia (where many had been landed during the war) and then proceeding to what became New Brunswick and finally to Upper Canada, or travelling through New York State and across the St Lawrence, the Loyalists who remained in North America (a number of them went to the West Indies) were Americans. British North Americans, yes, but Americans – the defeated in a vicious civil war. The scars of that defeat, and the binding-up of its wounds by the imperial authorities would produce a pervasive allegiance to the crown as well as a dependence upon it. It would also generate a deep dislike for the crown's enemies in the culture, the alternative anglophone culture, that the Loyalists would help to produce upon the North American continent.

V

However lengthy have been my background remarks on the intensity, pain, and confusion of the Loyalist war experience, the discussion must be prolonged to include another set of wartime tales. The events of 1812–15 loomed as important in the Loyalist view of their history as did those of the Revolution. What was once lost – the dignity of successfully defending one's own – was regained.

The colony of Upper Canada whose remote origins lay in catastrophe had experienced undramatic beginnings. Loyalists had pressed into Nova Scotia to find a civil and military establishment scarcely ready to receive them in the numbers they were or the style they had hoped for. The newcomers soon began to squabble with the residents over the allocation of offices and appointments, a pressure which produced the partitioning of the province in 1784 with the new unit, New Brunswick, set aside as a domain for Loyalist place-hunting. The Loyalists who first landed along the Bay of Quinte in what was to become Upper Canada (it was then Quebec) on 16 June 1784 were no less dependent than the Maritimers on imperial patronage. Indeed, they entered a hinterland more barren of their culture and its comforts than the Maritimes.[22] Fortunately, no hostile Indian tribes occupied the area, and the Mohawks to the west (near what is now Brantford) were themselves Loyalist refugees from the Six Nations.

As far as proved possible, the settlers were grouped by the authorities according to the units with which they had shared the experience of war. Thus, for example, units of Highland Scots came to settle in the Glengarry area of what is now eastern Ontario. This had been the initial policy in the Maritimes. It not only kept together groups who had shared experiences beyond those of being refugees, but also left intact the system of command and deference that military life necessitated and that the authorities thought should mark civilian life. The Loyalists had not lost everything to descend to becoming levelling republicans. Swords can be beaten into plowshares with greater ease than men used to the excitement, boredom, and irresponsibility of war can be turned into farmers and labourers. The necessity, however, for this kind of transformation was even more acute in Upper Canada than in Nova Scotia. The harbour at Halifax was the strongpoint of a maritime empire's presence in North America; government patronage would form the backbone of its economy for some time to come. Upper Canada's strategic importance lay in its role as a buffer zone which might offer a threat to a republic intent upon capturing the St Lawrence valley. No important military establishment was to arise there, and the civil establishment would only be commensurate with whatever increases in prosperity and population the colony brought about for itself.

The romantic movement, and chiefly the historical romances of Sir Walter Scott, would soon make poetic the plight of the loser, the colourful refugee torn from his former existence and plunged into a harsher one. Despite the Glengarry Scots, however, the founders of Upper Canada were not all kilted Jacobites; instead they were mostly poor farmers who had lost the fruits of their labours in the republic but whose labours had never yielded any great return.[23] Upper Canada was the frontier, a place with a better soil and growing climate than Nova Scotia, a place where those who had felt squeezed in the Maritimes and Quebec could establish themselves. By 1784, it struck the imperial authorities that Quebec would be better off as a French, Catholic domain (with a Protestant-dominated mercantile and governing élite). Those English-speaking farmers who wanted their own laws (especially about land tenure), customs, and representative assemblies would be better advised to found their own society along a frontier.

And so they did, in the face of all the hardships – land clearance, loneliness, climate, the necessity for unceasing labour – that their allegiance to the crown had laid on them. Though the crown furnished an initial stake of tools, seed grain, and supplies, not everyone possessed sufficient skills and luck to succeed. The fragile nature of the new colony was shown in the hungry year of 1788–9, a time of scarcity mentioned with abhorrence by settlers in account after account.

Still they persisted, and in 1791 Upper Canada was separated from Quebec and officially founded. While their first governor, the cavalryman John Graves Simcoe, attempted to make a little England out of the colony, the settlers adapted themselves to its wilderness and stark, roadless immensities. Governor Simcoe may have anglicized the map so that it read 'York' where once 'Toronto' appeared and Chippawa Creek became the Welland River. Yet the supply of loyal, anglicized colonists was limited. The new colony needed muscle from wherever it could be found – from former rebels even. He accordingly offered land grants to Americans willing to take an oath of allegiance. (By 1794, even this test of loyalty had been dropped.) In the event of trouble with the republic, those who did not consider themselves bound in heaven would surely be bound by their earthly ties in not wishing to have their lands invaded, even by their erstwhile brothers. By 1812, American immigration (late Loyalists) had swelled the colony, but its Loyalist founders numbered only 20 per cent of the population.[24] The events of that year thrust Upper Canada into the furnace of history, and subsequent historians reshaped the events of that time aided by the foundry of myth.

Upper Canada survived the war, chiefly through the ineptitude of American strategists, who kept grabbing their opponent about his Upper Canadian chest when they could so easily have clamped their fingers around his Montreal jugular. The triumph also came about through the energy, vision, and bravery of Sir Isaac Brock and his British regulars and the efforts of the local militia. They frustrated American attempts to conquer and occupy Upper Canada, though the capital was burnt and the western counties ravaged. The Loyalists congratulated themselves on successfully heartening the timid and curbing the traitorous among the population of Upper

Canada.[25] Under a leader they made into a mythic hero, they had emerged as the citizen defenders of their territory. An effective, energetic tactician and organizer, Brock, unlike the mercurial Wolfe, was a figure of little personal colour, a good soldier who became by his death at Queenston Heights a martyr to the principles of justice and the preservation of British North America.[26] The militia of Upper Canada, rather than the British regulars who formed the basis of Brock's holding strategy, became joined with Brock as the chief factors in the preservation of Upper Canada. John Graves Simcoe had led a unit of Loyalist citizen-soldiers, so it was no great trick for pious memorialists to remove Brock's regulars from his command and substitute the provincial militia. No one denied the role of the professionals; instead came a shift in emphasis that bruised historical fact in placing another group in the forefront of the fight.[27]

The result of 1812–15 was a typical Loyalist victory: no glorious triumph through the enemy's capital (though British regulars burnt it in retaliation for the torching of York), no acquisition of fame and booty, but instead survival, a victory of grit and endurance. Its most important effect lay in the shape it gave the Loyalist myth, for that took on the configuration of the Christian process of agony, defeat, and resurrection. Unlike what happened in the Maritimes, history supplied Upper Canada with a military component to the Loyalist heritage. Thus, even a pastoral myth of Upper Canada, like that behind William Kirby's *The U.E.*, would contain a military threat and confirm in blood the strength of the covenant. The very fact of survival vindicated Loyalist principles. Defeated in their first test, the Loyalists had not been found wanting in the second. The anonymous saving remnant with a martyred hero at their head had guaranteed that Upper Canada was to remain an imperial headland jutting upon a republican sea.[28]

VI

So rich a myth carried with it political ramifications. The Reverend John Strachan and his associates in the colonial oligarchy known as the Family Compact wielded mightily this fabular sword. Many of the élite's members had not arrived as Loyalists but as British immigrants to Upper Canada, though it is fair to say that just as many came as the younger sons of established Maritime Loyalist families.[29] They made themselves conspicuous during the hostilities in their efforts to rally the population. Leaders of the resistance, active in the judicial terror that had kept the wavering in line (see

n. 25), they had Strachan as a guide. He had shouldered the burden of negotiating the surrender of York to an angry American fighting force. Loyalty rather than Loyalism became the oligarchs' watchword; the two words sounded close enough for the élite to appear as the colony's founders. Their rhetoric, the formulas they employed for purging their enemies, emphasized that it was they themselves who were particularly loyal, particularly elect, with social dissenters easily labelled as disloyal American-izers of the colony.[30] Strict accountability of the governors to the governed, a free press, some slight bow in the direction of merit (or even towards the principle of some share in the pie for every group) as a criterion for the distribution of offices: these could be branded as American, levelling aims. In a perverse, ironic fashion, the colony had been saddled with a would-be aristocracy and a would-be established church that Simcoe had never been able to install officially. The events leading up to 1837 and the overthrow of that élite at its moment of triumph need not be rehearsed here. What counts is that 1776 and 1812 became bands upon a single spectrum of Loyalist clashes with republicanism in North America.

The war of 1812 may have been instrumental in the creation of a distinctive Upper Canadian culture. Still, the oligarchy exacted a heavy political price in making what it called Loyalism into a strait-jacket for the colony. William Lyon Mackenzie and his followers eventually came to the point of seeking to hand Upper Canada over to the Americans. Surely they arrived there not out of a perverse hatred of British institutions, but because an intransigent provincial oligarchy had denied them the representative institutions that British colonists had come to look on as their right. A definition of loyalty that meant subservience to a corrupt regime could not help but induce in future Upper Canadians an equation of United Empire Loyalism with the failings of that regime.

VII

Enough of the élitist sleight-of-hand by which loyalty was equated with Loyalism. What of the value of the Loyalist myth in organizing Upper Canada's sense of itself? Egerton Ryerson's pious history of Upper Canadian Loyalism, *The Loyalists of America and their times* (1880) gives us an idea of this. The 1884 centennial celebrations of the first Loyalist landings along the Bay of Quinte were a grand occasion for the retelling of the myth in the much loved tropes of public oratory, and Ryerson's work can be seen as the opening chant in the service of thanksgiving.[31] Ryerson, Methodist and Clear Grit, felt no affection for the Anglican, reactionary ethos of the Family Compact. None the less, his history presented the mythic union between 1776 and 1812 that had served so well interests contrary to his own.[32] Himself of Loyalist stock, he had collected materials for two decades before publishing his book.[33] Unable to impose any firm structure upon his material, the author at times drowns in a sea of lengthy quotations. As has been said of another, 'he may have run out of energy and found it easier to become a compiler – a familiar historical tradition in British North America.'[34] The work's value lies in its collection of first-hand settler accounts and in its function as a repository of the Loyalist myth.

If there were such a thing as a Loyalist mentality, one aspect of it would have been a certain hesitancy about acknowledging one's American roots. A person may overcompensate for the similarity of his origins to his opponent's by denying any eventual resemblance. Yet one of the reasons that the Loyalists lost the Revolutionary war was that initially they shared their fellow countrymen's misgivings about the course the imperial government appeared to be taking. Not only militant levellers and republicans disagreed with the government's policies on colonial manufactures. From holding that opinion to picking up a gun is a longer step than the John Strachans of this world would have it. It wrongs the Loyalists to view them as gravitating by nature to the 'establishment'-mindedness that members of the Family Compact claimed to be the mark of decently governed people. Their first churches in Upper Canada were not Church of England (with all the High Tory associations later implied in that confession) but Roman Catholic, Lutheran, and Methodist. The finest of them (St Andrew's, Williamstown) was erected by Scots Presbyterians, and even Strachan's first church (Holy Trinity, Cornwall) was built in the austere New England style by craftsmen from that region.[35] The Loyalists first and foremost wanted nothing to do with what they considered the disorderliness, the militant democracy of u.s. government and society. This had not however made them pine for a church and aristocracy. They could be appealed to on the basis of a throne-and-altar High Toryism, but that idealization of the monarchy and religion-as-a-bulwark-of-society is a far cry from longing for a mandarinate.

All this leads up to Ryerson's attitudes toward the Puritans. Puritans played no small part in letting English monarchs know that they had a joint in their necks. An alteration in power arrangements, rather than sweet reason, extended to some Englishmen the liberties the Americans enshrined in the first ten amendments to their constitution. Ryerson's opening at once praises the civil liberties and responsible government Canada enjoys and contrasts the

Pilgrims with the Puritans, to the detriment of the latter. His partisanship obscures for him the Puritan role in obtaining these liberties. In an effort to distinguish 'good,' inner-light libertarians (Pilgrims) from 'bad,' rebellious totalitarians (Puritan), Ryerson ignores the linkage between his ancestors, their enemies, and the system he praises.

The understandable wish to repudiate the u.s. that had so roughly handled the Loyalists and to exalt the post-confederation reality of Canada kept Ryerson from coming to grips with the complex nature of his own heritage. That failure cannot be confined to Ryerson and his times alone. It is a permanent feature of our cultural life. Although it would be folly to blame the Loyalists for our attempt to harden what are at times fluid distinctions, Ryerson's history shows what many have made of Loyalism and what over the years has come to seem an aspect of the Loyalist mentality. Ryerson's search for a foe beyond the walls of the garrison makes him skirt closely a conspiracy theory of the American Revolution, employing terms like 'a clique of Congregational Republicans and Separationists' to describe some of the members of the Continental Congress. He who fights dragons becomes one; polemicists on both sides attribute to either royalist plotters or republican conspirators the origins of the Revolution.[36]

Perhaps the fate of all actual Loyalists, then and since, remains that of seeking to occupy some middle ground between clashing fanaticisms. Ryerson's difficulty is that he cannot call attention to a clumsiness on the part of the imperial ministry without also having to bring forward some derogatory remarks on the nature of the ministry's opponents (1: 347–8, 431–2). In steering this course he must perforce neglect his own people, so that the reader gains a sense of the Loyalists only as a vague, ill-defined mass who managed to discern the follies of George III without falling prey to the rantings of a Sam Adams. Ryerson himself ironically makes the same error as the original Loyalists, turning over the stage to his opponents out of insensitivity to the need to explain his own beliefs. In fact, the writings of a nineteenth century American historian, Lorenzo M. Sabine (the first u.s. historian who tried to discover exactly who the despised, exiled Tories were), provide a better portrait than Ryerson's of the Loyalists themselves. To feel defensive can produce introspection as well as bombast, and Sabine puts to good use his 'minority role' as an American historian.[37]

Ryerson's history includes the events of the war of 1812 and in so doing displays the contours of the Loyalist myth. Mere fact – 'the American settlers in Canada were, with few exceptions, as loyal subjects and as bold defenders of their country as the u.e. Loyalists' – even when dutifully acknowledged, cannot suppress the mythic utterance: 'The true spirit of the *Loyalists of America* was never exhibited with greater force and brilliancy than during the

War of 1812–15' (ii: 316–17). Though the history consists largely of unpruned citations from various historians, authorial comments sink home the text's message: 'The Spartan bands of Canadian Loyalist volunteers, aided by a few hundred English soldiers and civilized Indians, repelled the Persian thousands of democratic American invaders ...' (ii: 379). That kind of classical imagery was typically associated with American republicanism; in this instance it has been appended to an account of a few, relatively minor skirmishes which repelled some final, ill-planned American invasion efforts in the Niagara area. The grandeur of the remarks far exceeds that of the occasion (in this, it resembles Simcoe's war journals), but the diction reveals the mythic frame enclosing events.

Since Ryerson's work is actually a tribal lay rather than a modern history, it sums up 1812 in a patriotic address he delivered at Brock's Momument on Queenston Heights during an anniversary celebration of the battle of Lundy's Lane which is reprinted in his history. Here the militia again takes the leading role. The speech conveys how the rhetoric of a generation of romantic historians like Michelet, glorifiers of the *levée en masse* during the wars of the French Revolution, finds itself echoed in the remarks of a provincial memorialist. Virgil had supplied the western mind with one pattern for the Loyalist experience, with America the burning Troy and Canada as Latium. Sir Walter Scott's evocations of a vanished feudal Scotland had decked out defeated minorities in gorgeous robes. Now theories of popular and mass sovereignty, however alien and remote, gave to 1812 the aura of a people's war. The final mixture bubbles away as a characteristic nineteenth century blend of Christianity and romanticism. Virgil, marmoreal yet prophetic, served as an adjunct to both. The despised minority became a saving remnant, and the stout-hearted pilgrim-refugees an exemplar of the collective heroism and strength to be found in the common people. That kind of heroic-democratic image would be more explicitly articulated in a u.s. popular, polemical historian such as George Bancroft, but it lies slumbering here as well, in the spokesman for Loyalist Ontario.

VIII

Historians agree that their expulsion left the Loyalists with an abiding distrust of the u.s. and its political institutions. In addition, it gave them a willingness to place public order above all competing political values. The crown, un-American and the guarantor of Pax Britannica, embodied these values and thus became the UEL totem.[38] These marks of a deeply frustrating and embittering experience were common to all Canadian Loyalists, though the Upper Canadian experience, as we have seen, added some particular features to the more generalized effects. The adoption of 1812 as an integral part of the Loyalist self-image and history meant that an element of vindication had been added to the chronicle of suffering and injustice. Indeed, in public oratory that vindication could be inflated into triumph. To the Christian sensibility, this made for a perfect symmetry; Christianity and romance melded as the familiar folkloric motif of the despised-shown-as-best appeared. As well, the romantic cultural creed that swept the west at the beginning of the nineteenth century could view these exiles with particular affection both as outcasts (like Scottish Highlanders, deserted mothers, vagabonds, minstrels, etc.) and as intrepid citizen-defenders of a threatened state (Horatius, William Tell, Judas Maccabeus). An optimistic pattern had been salvaged from tragic material. Of course, that symbolic pattern of experience, that historical vindication, required the righteous never to have lingered in the fleshpots of Egypt. That in turn made it difficult to acquire a realistic sense of the Loyalists' relationship to their former country. It also meant that genuine tragedy could not arise out of their departure from that one-time home, since tragedy involves ultimately a vision of man destroyed not merely by outside powers but also by the tendencies and inconsistencies he carries within himself. Instead, reality had to be divided into good and evil forces. Nature, for example, might have to be viewed as a cruel or at least an indifferent force against which man contends in vain; the humane aspects of culture might come to be seen as fragile defences against a world of extreme savagery that could only be dealt with from inside a defended enclosure. In such instances, irony – the grim realization that something 'outside,' yet garbed in the most 'inside' of guises, was forever waiting to pounce – would substitute for tragedy. The prospects for group survival would appear sounder than any hope of individual enhancement. An outlook shuttling between extemes of individual irony and collective optimism could rarely find room for a reasonably fulfilled individual. Either he would be a communal hero whose value lay in his representative nature, or some battered individual struck down by the inexorableness of inexorability. Mere contradictory liveliness would never suffice.

The following two chapters probe the appearance of these consequences in two contrasting writers who shed considerable light on the cultural preoccu-pations derived in part from the Loyalist legacy. 'And without shedding of blood is no remission,' defines the world views that lie beneath the surface of their writings; it determines the painful nature of the destinies imposed upon their imaginary characters.

2 *William Kirby and the Garden*

> For the Lord shall comfort Zion: he will comfort all her waste places;
> and he will make her wilderness like Eden, and her desert like the
> garden of the Lord; joy and gladness shall be found therein, thanks-
> giving, and the voice of melody – Isaiah 51: 3

> So prepared for doing the work of Evangelists, we may, with holy
> boldness, look forward to the time when the whole Province will be-
> come the garden of the Lord – John Strachan, 'Charge to the diocesan
> clergy,' 1841

William Kirby (1817–1906) gave us a vision of Upper Canada as a garden,
with its special covenantal status confirmed through the blood spilled in
historical conflicts. Yet his readers need also to remember the eighteenth-
century iconographic tradition by which the painting of a garden contained
somewhere a tomb bearing the legend, Et In Arcadia Ego (freely translated,
And I am here, even in Arcadia). The neo-classical era's equivalent to a
medieval *memento mori* is implicit in Kirby's new Eden. In his historical
romance, *The golden dog*, a loyal Canada must live with the fear that colonial
fidelity may not be reciprocated by the mother country. Kirby's epic of Upper
Canada, *The U.E.*, includes the grim corollaries to the proposition that the
covenant must be preserved – the hardening of social affections through
protracted violence, the sacrifice of youth in war. Kirby's Canada, garden and
garrison, stands both troubled and triumphant.

Author of *The U.E.* and 'The United Empire Loyalists of Canada,' featured
speaker at the Bay of Quinte and Niagara UEL centennial celebrations, subject
of a biography subtitled 'Portrait of a Tory Loyalist,' the man who referred to
himself as 'the last of the Loyalists' did not come of an Upper Canadian
background. He had been born the son of a Yorkshire tanner, whom business
reverses sent to the U.S. in 1832. Kirby's great-grandmother had fled back to
England from Virginia at the outbreak of the Revolutionary war, which did
not stop her descendants from settling in Cincinnati, Ohio. There Kirby
stayed until 1839. Not until then did he arrive in Upper Canada with the
vague resolve 'to go to Canada and aid in the defence of the Provinces.'[1] That
sense of mission was outlined in a pamphlet at a distance of forty years. His
biographer ventures no further. His assimilation into Upper Canada was not
immediate. He first journeyed to Toronto, Quebec, and Montreal and then

returned to what was to be lifelong residence at Niagara-on-the-Lake. It seems reasonable to suppose that his marriage there in 1847 to Eliza Madaline Whitmore provided him with a ready-made clan of Loyalists within the district and quickened his memory of his great-grandmother, who had always assured him that the Loyalists had been the best people in Virginia.[2]

There is a compensatory quality to Kirby's quasi-professional Loyalism. Born elsewhere, too lately arrived in Upper Canada to have participated in its confessional armed struggles, the largely self-educated tanner bought a newspaper with his wife's money. Cultivating himself in formidable fashion, he found in his Loyalist ancestry and marital connection a ready-made social niche.[3] He was to describe himself as having entered Canada bearing a rifle in order to defend it against its enemies; his self-definition lay in his role as a defender of an alien Old Order. The idea of Loyalism, which he equated both with Toryism and fidelity in general, offered him a ghostly paradigm according to which nearly every sort of social and political situation could be defined. As late as 1891, we find him writing to Colonel George T. Denison of a federal election in which Sir John A. Macdonald's struggle against the Grits assumes the shape of a Loyalist struggle with a revolutionary conspiracy; Macdonald, 'like Brock,' goes forth 'to asail his enemy in the new Detroit.' Kirby draws out the extravagant figure of speech even further: 'We have to fight on for Canada, do not let us Loyalists be submissive and timid as were the Loyalists at the beginning of the revolution of 1775, and allow the other side to organize and take the lead before we begin to vindicate our rights and resolution to live as British citizens even to the extent of blood.'[4] This seems a far cry from the pork-barrel banality of a Canadian election; that over-heated rhetoric would have disturbed Sara Jeannette Duncan's Elgin, Ontario, rather more than did the gentle, idealistic imperialism of Lorne Murchison. Kirby's imperial idealism was not the New Imperialism of markets and trade agreements. It rested rather on a sense of Loyalism as a way of life, a conviction whose origins lay in a covenant in which right and successful living enjoined an utter devotion to the culture and mission of the mother country.[5]

Despite his associations with Denison and his membership in the Imperial Federation League, despite his Orange Ontario fanaticism that made him treasure as a souvenir a piece of the rope that had hanged Riel, he differs from Canada First in that a sense of nationalism never arose in his writings. Neither in their message nor in their literary form do they attempt to accommodate the experience of Canada.[6] Not for him the vision of Canada as an independent nation gaining greater resonance through its imperial context. Allegiance to Britain was sufficient in itself. 'He was an Englishman before a Canadian and … the authentic Canadian … literary note … would probably have irritated and alienated him.'[7] His anglophone heroes, as the author of the above quotation noted, remain without exception UEL or British. Other and wider possibilities for Canada failed to attract him.

That consideration will remain throughout the writers studied here. Two varying perceptions of Loyalism's relationship to nationalism prevail. The first would assert that the maintenance of the historical ties to Britain offers the only firm basis for a genuine nationalism, because the links are not simply to Britain, but to the entire tradition of western civility. Traditions, modes of behaviour, the thousand unknowing fashions in which we confirm our own roots, these are not Platonic entities absorbed by communion with the ideal. They arise bearing local names in small places. Thus the Loyalist case, thus the British imperial/commonwealth case for Canada's mode of connecting to the greater good.

A second view of Canadian nationalism would emphasize the incompatibility of it with any great concern over the Loyalist experience. Such a view holds that a concern with the fact of Loyalism entails an accompanying anglophilia that keeps our gaze focused on matters obsolete, irrelevant, and elsewhere. It forces a distortion of Canadian and North American realities. A version of nationalism intent upon our British origins turns the nation into a club, giving to other groups – both earlier and later arrivals – a second-class status. Certainly much of what lies in this essay may sadden, in that readers can observe these Loyalist visions cramping any wider sense of our destiny.

Granting that, we must still ask ourselves where we are most likely to find any sense of Canada as part of a greater, more noble company of states extending back into the origins of the western world. Will we find it through a generalized sense of the brotherhood of man, or in a sharp perception of our own historical roots? Even when one admits what this essay reveals, that the Loyalist vision of Upper Canada and Canada in general has at times substituted manners for substance, tragic posturing for agonized conviction, and hierarchy for brotherhood, the question still stands. Even if we do not always like our history, must we not come to terms with it? These matters arise, but they extend beyond any discussion of Kirby in particular. They loom over the entire study, even if the questions they raise cannot be answered here.

Despite the narrowness of his ideas about the nature of Canadian culture, Kirby's vision of Canada possesses the universal appeal of pastoralism. The violence that threatens his peaceable kingdom never occurs outside a host of forms and usages that explain and civilize it. The wilderness yields gracefully to the efforts of the pioneer, who comes not to release himself from the bonds of civilization but to forge them in a new setting. Kirby's archaic verse forms, which so ruthlessly fit the most potentially subversive happenings into a tight framework of accountability and control, resemble his vision of the meaning of Loyalism, which like some celestial sausage machine, grinds order out of disharmony and affirmation from disaster.[8]

While the violence in Kirby's writing remains spasmodic – rather than serving as an abiding condition of existence, as in the works of Major Richardson – some of it does recall the grisliness of Richardson's *Wacousta*. For example, one of the major events of this novel, the betrayal of Pontiac's plans to an officer of the Detroit garrison by his Indian paramour, forms the centre of Kirby's 'Pontiac.'[9] *The U.E.* tells of an heroic white who, maddened by the rebels' massacre of his family, dons Indian garb and wages a savage guerilla campaign in the Mohawk valley. Based on an historical figure, Captain John Clement, 'Ranger John' comes close to cannibalism when he eats the bread – stained with an enemy's blood – that he has filched from a foeman's knapsack.[10] The reader can imagine one of Richardson's ghouls working his way up from bread to head, but that sort of thing never gets out of hand in Kirby. The claims of decency are reasserted. Ranger John, even when crazed enough to try to kill his traitorous son, finds his savagery displaced again as the young man falls to a stray bullet.

Atrocities are blunted and subversion quelled because Kirby's Upper Canada is not wilderness but garden. Loyalty at once created the garden and makes it endure.

I

The U.E. (1859) is an epic of twelve cantos, composed in stanzas of from six to thirteen heroic couplets apiece. It extends the Loyalist thirty years' war (or even forty years: 1775–1815) by another two decades. The events of 1837 become another Loyalist conflict, recapitulating the familiar struggle against traitors and foreign invaders. Ranger John links these struggles together. Kirby places 1837 and all its complexities within the simplistic framework of yet another attempt at the subversion of monarchical loyalty. Nothing is accidental about the poem's dedication to John Beverley Robinson, the dean of the ruling élite who found so congenial that black and white view of the struggle.

The epic's martyred hero, Ethwald, while seen as a Loyalist, is less of one than Kirby himself. Walwyn, Ethwald's father, arrived in Upper Canada from England after 1812. Loyalism here is a talismanic term, set free from its historical and socio-political roots. Loyalism becomes a state of mind equated with loyalty itself. That, in turn, is equated with an unyielding conservatism. Think of it as a title granted to bearers of archaic, Anglo-Saxon names who appear willing to pick up a gun to defend the status quo. Ranger John, the actual UEL, stands as but one in a group of virtual UELs, those granted the title retrospectively as a reward for political allegiance. After all, the ranger's son, Hugh, may be a malevolent traitor but his claim to be a UEL rests on far firmer ground than that of Walwyn or Ethwald since he was born of a Loyalist parent. The term has shifted from the definitional to the sacramental, becoming in passage what we now call a buzz-word, a signal that its subject commends approbation and respect.

The setting itself functions as a grouping of pastoral motifs bearing a number of symbolic, traditional overtones. It is far from an actual, meticulously observed landscape. The introductory stanzas make the obligatory references to Virgil, the epic and imperial Virgil.[11] The Maro of the *Georgics* and *Eclogues*, that patient observer of rural ways never appears here, unless as one of the sources of a number of images of rustic life that had become shopworn long before Kirby began to write. The epic's title-page bears as its colophon the image of a beehive, but not the sort of homely beehive a farmer may have garnered honey from. This hive symbolizes the happy polity, the state of hierarchy, cooperation, and distilled sweetness. *The U.E.* views Upper Canadian life through these clichés (or traditional figures) and with their distancing effect.

Our first glimpse of one of the characters, therefore, finds him 'scythe in hand, / With rural triumph head[ing] the rustic band' (canto 1: stanza 3). Why rustic, wherefore rural? Upper Canada still had far to go in attaining its roaring, metropolitan, strip-development apotheosis, but the metropolitan reality these adjectives contrast with lies not in Toronto or Kingston, but in London or Manchester. Only in terms of the implicit colonial situation can these hinterlanders appear as 'lithe,' 'sun-burnt' rustics. And this is how they cheerfully see themselves, these residents and defenders of what Kirby will call repeatedly 'the Forest Land.' Those very trees will attain their highest purpose when they rise 'sublime' as masts from the decks of British warships (2: 21).

The mention of the forest land brings us to the idea of the garden that so permeates this poem. That may seem paradoxical, but Kirby's forest grows worlds away from Richardson's, at an imaginative distance far greater than that between Niagara and Detroit. In the context of the poem, 'forest' roams somewhat free from its usual connotations. It is not Blake's forest of the night, but the Forest of Arden, a spot distanced from disloyalty and disaffection. The events of the poem move like sleepwalkers through a symbolic landscape in which the common stuff of reality nestles peacefully amid an ambience that everywhere enhances it:

The riders ...
Survey the glorious landscape spread below.
A sea of forests that for ages grew;
And belts of open, where the axe passed through;
With fields and farmsteads veiled in night's soft pall,
And church and mill that rise distinct from all. (9: 29)

Sacred and secular alike blend easily into their charming surroundings.

An earlier, topographical section of the poem repeats prosaically that symbolic journey into the belly of the whale that Frye has caught as an archetypal venture of the Canadian consciousness.[12] Ethwald and Walwyn sail along the riverain artery of the peaceable kingdom, with the Citadel at Quebec appearing amid its natural surroundings 'like Mars reposing in fair Venus' arms' (2: 7), to arrive at a scriptural setting near the source of the St Lawrence. The green pastures of the Psalmist (2: 29) rest amid a river valley itself serving as a latter-day Arcadia (2: 19). The journey toward the garden extends to another canto, where the announcement of a dawning golden age precedes the sighting of Lake Ontario. This juxtaposition of moral vision with topography hints at the paradisal qualities of Upper Canada: the Arcadian image swells at the mention of the vineyards of the Niagara peninsula (3: 17).

Amid this profusion of symbolic scenery, the immigrants begin their task of gardening the forest land. Arcadia and the green pastures do not arise effortlessly, and we have glimpsed the hint of a snake in the garden earlier on. The narratives of the Loyalists themselves showed some unease at growing prosperity and technological progress; they appeared as temptations to abandon the rugged virtue of earlier times.[13] Kirby's poem locates in the steamship the impress of a moving age, but it also notes the dangerous figures of the serpent and the tree of knowledge. The following stanza then shudders at the thought – familiar after Keats' distrust of 'cold philosophy' in *Lamia* – that science may strip life of its spiritual and poetic aspects (3: 3–4).

These hints of trouble, though they are mild enough never to challenge seriously the poem's idealized optimism, account for Walwyn's fears over his ability to clear the land. Doubts soon give way to hopeful thoughts and communal prayer, yet the poem cannot shake these anxieties fully. For the prayer's conclusion heralds the arrival of Ranger John. At first he seems the sort of old man as natural spirit found in Wordsworth's 'Resolution and

Independence,' but he soon establishes himself as the troubled figure whose career of deprivation and revenge I have already mentioned. In fact, the threat Ranger John poses to the Arcadian vision of Upper Canada preoccupies the two-thirds of the poem that remain.

The vengeful obsessions of this figure get at a truth about the Loyalist mind that the poem heretofore avoided. Fairies incongruously disported themselves at the opening of the third canto, creatures even less appropriate here than those happy rural swains mentioned previously. These Old World transplants cannot survive amid the grim accounts of betrayal, massacre, and border warfare with which Ranger John regales the settlers. He not only welcomes them to their new homeland with his woodsman's lore, but also begins to acclimatize them to the Richardsonian realities of their happy rural seat. Then, his account of a seven-year war concluded, the skirmisher – almost as if the years of terror had vanished without trace – describes in glowing terms the new life he has made in the forest land.

Of course, that is not so. The next canto shows how much disturbance underlies the pastoral tranquillity. The surly Hugh appears; he is not only a sore loser after a wrestling match with Ethwald, but the sort of blackguard who would seek his fortune in the Babylon to the south (5: 8–10, 14–15). Hugh will go on to slay his brother while leading an American raiding party in 1837 and himself die later, nearly at the hands of his father, in the skirmish at Crysler's Farm.

No need to become lost in the story, whose importance lies in its presentation of a set of experiences mocking the pastoral model imposed upon the setting. Those fairies that canto three transported to the valley of the St Lawrence behave like the fey, elfin folk of the painter Francis Danby. In view of the experiences of Ranger John, those fairies could better have stepped from the canvas of Richard William Dadd. Deformed, lubricious, grotesquely arrayed, the creatures in 'The fairy-feller's master stroke' would closer suit the accounts presented of betrayal and barbarity.

Lest the threat to serenity presented by Hugh and his father loom too large in the reader's imagination, the author soon shifts to a description of the self-sufficient pioneer home, crammed with naturally finished wood and home-made objects:

The plenteous, cleanly, warm Canadian home.
Massive and strong, each household good displayed
The simple truthfulness their minds arrayed.
Well-cushioned chairs of solid oaken wood,
And heavy tables firm and squarely stood;

> While female taste, from needle, wheel and loom
> With cheerful drapery adorned each room.
> Upon the heavy beams dependent swung
> Crooked powder-horns, and well-kept rifles hung;
> And by the massive chimney's deep recess,
> Huge antlers held the hunter's sylvan dress.
> Upon the table lay with reverent care,
> The family bible and the book of prayer (5: 21)

This attempt to restore the Golden Age works itself with difficulty through the rest of the poem. Canto six celebrates seven years of peace as it describes an Edenic landscape and sings the praises of homespun cloth (6: 19, 26). It also retells the story of Daphne and Apollo in Amerindian terms, concluding a motif of cultural transmission in which a Canadian Virgil retells the classics in Indian dress. Once this interlude has passed and a following canto packs Ethwald back to England to pick up the girl he left behind, rebellion and invasion occupy the poem's attention until its conclusion.

These sections depict Walwyn and Ethwald's growing realization of the bloodthirstiness of the genius of the place, Ranger John. The brutality of his years of combat cannot be wiped away. The man is a ranting killer who can only with difficulty be talked out of slaying his traitorous son, whose infidelity to the king the old man loathes more than the boy's filial disobedience (5: 11, 10: 31–2). As stated earlier, Hugh's death happens by way of a stray bullet rather than through his father's upraised tomahawk, but the death of the noble Ethwald makes sense only as a surrogate to atone for the filial rebellion that has taken place.

This emphasis on violence is reflected in the poem's structure as well as in its content. In structure the poem typically delivers a series of moral-topograph-ical-historical 'background' stanzas before moving to a tableau in which is captured a moment of action: a wrestling match, a raid, a dance, and so forth. Kirby spares no epic figure in inflating Crysler's Farm to Homeric proportions. That struggle concluded, the final scene composes itself into a cameo of the two fathers – Ranger John with his sons now dead, Walwyn a benign grandpa living with the family of his dead son – declaiming about loyalty and patriotism. Pull that scene from its lulling context and it offers a shocking reversal of a sacrificial motif; here the old men have watched their sons slain and now comfortably eke out their own lives mumbling justifica-tions for those deaths. Filial piety, that emblem of loyalty, exacts a one-sided payment, since the price of rebellion entails the removal of an entire generation.

This sort of ruthlessness within an Edenic setting recalls the ferocity of the Niagara Loyalist families who went about digging up the bones of the rebels and 'sympathizers' who lay buried in their turf, an occurrence that provides a grisly-jocular interlude during the *Canadian idylls*.[14] Loyalism and Loyalists scarcely held a monopoly on the image of Upper Canada as a garden, as Strachan's epigraph to this chapter and the writings of Mrs Moodie attest.[15] Kirby's garden gains its unique flavour from the large number of snakes that must be routed continually from it. His *Annals of Niagara*, a shapeless historical narrative, offers a procession of the seditious and fifth columnists, of loyalty oaths and the expulsion of the disaffected. We also watch the growth of savagery as the border war of 1812 degenerates into terror and counter-terror.[16] Surprisingly for a man like Kirby who was not there, who could be expected to bring some measure of objectivity to his observation of the past, the witch hunt is never linked with the brutal warfare as another mark of wartime nastiness. Instead, once the invader has been repelled or scotched, the gardeners can return to their idyllic state without any need for self-examination. All remains well until the next danger presents itself, while the maintenance of the Loyalist covenant will insure the crushing of that threat.

This pattern of the embattled paradise arises again in 'The hungry year,' one of the *Canadian idylls*. Though composed later, it presents a miniature thematic version of *The U.E.* Here the garden is initially wrenched from a state of raw nature and its existence affirmed. A frightful event (the death of a farming couple by starvation) conflicts with the Arcadian vision, which is then newly reaffirmed when the death itself purges whatever evil once marked the spot. The garden flourishes again as the poem's attention shifts from the dead and focuses on the grand, patriotic future under the authority of the crown.

This reworking of a Christian redemptive pattern so as to avoid any sense of tragedy entails the use of literary convention as a means of disregarding the subversive implications of the subject. Kirby exploited a set of pastoral figures whose very origins gave them little to do with the experience his poem purported to examine.

II

When, in 1877, Kirby came to publish an historical romance based on Canadian material (thus founding what was to be one of Canada's chief nineteenth-century export trades), he chose New France rather than the

Greater Britain of the UEL for his subject-matter. The change only demonstrates the ease with which Kirby employed the conventions of the historical novel to impose on the history of New France the same covenantal pattern he had located in Upper Canada. A romantic culture's fascination with lost causes, the glamour of the *ancien régime*, the heroism of priests and soldiers: these are some of the factors generating New France's hold over the literary imagination, factors compelling the attention of any historical novelist in search of material. A large number of Francis Parkman's volumes on France and England in North America – histories that exploit to the full the devices of the historical novel – had appeared by the time *The golden dog* was published, and Kirby found his subject in a series on the historical byways of New France by the historical *feuilletoniste*, Sir James M. Le Moine. During an 1865 visit to Quebec, Kirby first came across Le Moine's essay on 'Le chien d'or: the history of an old house,' and years of research followed while Kirby swotted up the details of life in Canada under the *ancien régime*.[17] As a modern critic has noted, Kirby's efforts did not concern themselves with 'the French-Canadian life of his own times. Nor was it research on the realities of colonial or national politics of any time.'[18] Certainly that is true. What Kirby did produce was a romance that put forward another version of the moralistic, loyal Canada he had first shown in *The U.E.* Beneath all the glitter, lace, swordplay, curled lips, and operatic machinations of the novel lies a simplistic, tendentious, but coherent vision of a national destiny.

Nowhere does this quasi-tribalist preoccupation show itself more than in Kirby's alteration of his sources. The killing which forms the novel's climax led in real life to a feud ending in a duel fought along the sands of Pondicherry in France's falling Indian empire. Kirby chose to ignore what could have been a prize to any historical romancer. Instead he focuses exclusively on the New France from which he had expelled his characters, wanting no distraction from his national theme.

Indeed, who would wish to be distracted from a glimpse of Eden? It is from such a prospect that the novel opens its consideration of Quebec: 'Eternity would be too short to weary me of this lovely scene – this bright Canadian morning is worthy of Eden, and the glorious landscape worthy of such a sun rising.'[19] The structure of the work creates a number of polarities: the bourgeois Philibert, a trader and one of the *honnêtes gens*, stands in sharp contrast to the swindlers of *La Friponne* and its head, Intendant Bigot. Philibert's son, the soldier Pierre, serves in his manly sobriety as a foil to the goodhearted rakehell, the aristocratic Le Gardeur de Repentigny. The latter falls in love with Pierre's sister and in a drunken rage slays his love's father. The corruption and dazzle of the courtly Angélique are offset by the homely virtues of Amélie de Repentigny (the beloved, of course, of Pierre Philibert). The presence of starkly polarized characters in a piece of historical fiction should surprise no one. This sharp moral distinction between characters dovetails with a similar one in setting. The Edenic reference in the opening paragraph remains no casual figure of speech, but a consistent way of viewing an innocent New France in contrast to the corruptions of the Old.

In a chapter dropped from later editions of the novel, the first edition tells of an after-dinner conversation which ranges from the mists of Swedenborgian idealism to the diluvian reaches of Atlantis. The New World antedates the Old geologically, with its aboriginal inhabitants the oldest of mankind. Theirs are the earliest tongues, their Laurentian mountains the most ancient of ranges. Eventually the conversation reaches the real stuff of what used to be called the speculative mythographers – the kind of now-discarded but once-respectable theories that form so much of the intellectual background to *Middlemarch* – when Atlantis is named as a former North American civilization.[20] This catalogue of New World mythologies forms an especially rich context in which to place Philibert's garden-like estate of Belmont: 'A stately park, the remains of the primeval forest of oak, maple and pine; trees of gigantic growth and ample shade, surrounded the high-roofed, many-gabled house that stood on the heights of Ste. Foye overlooking the broad valley of the St. Charles. The bright river wound like a silver serpent through the flat meadows in the bottom of the valley ... ' (*Golden dog*, chap. xx, 196–7). Eden has appeared with a built-in snake in the form of a stream. The garden's primeval growth, tamed sufficiently by man to include a dwelling that rests in harmony with the benign forest, shows that the New World, which is in fact the elder, holds a purer form of human society. Something magical marks these country estates; when Le Gardeur returns to Tilly to escape the dissipations of Quebec, the manor house provides a place of peace and purity. From the beginning of his trip there, the songs of the voyageurs and the beauties of the landscape lift him from his jaded state (xxvi, 256ff.). Seigneurial ceremonies expressing the comforts of ritual and tradition mark the spot. Even the little nearby village offers the corruptions of drink; only the manor remains secure (xxviii, 275ff.). The 'good' couple, Pierre and Amélie, can plight their troth on the estate. When a crack of thunder portentously concludes their doomed vows, they repair to the manor house. There they rest 'safe under the protection of its strong and hospitable roof' (xxix, 295). These chapters set at Tilly occur almost halfway through the novel and provide a last time-out from the sequence of disasters that follows.

These calamities, unsurprisingly, come about when Old World crimes and intrigues intrude into the innocent New. To the commonplaces of traditional

Quebec nationalism – the betrayal of New France by the corrupt Old, which in turn paid for its crimes by the triumph of a godless revolution that forced France's soul to relocate in ultramontanist Quebec – Kirby adds a set of fictional events that make Old World corruption versus New World innocence the pivotal dichotomy of the many the novel contains.[21] The villains of the piece embody the worst excesses of Old France; in his domestic habits Bigot plans alien vices within a primeval setting: 'The Château seemed a very pandemonium of riot and revelry, that prolonged the night into the day, and defied the very order of nature by its audacious disregard of all decency of time, place and circumstance.'[22] Beaumanoir, Bigot's chateau, rivals Versailles in its extravagance and decadence. The schemes of Bigot and Angélique, his villainous and sexually compelling paramour, are twice described in terms of Versailles and the intrigues of Louis xv and Pompadour.[23] A girl whom Bigot ruins and then confines in his castle is of course a New World forest child. Bigot's very speech betrays him: his Parisian accent stands out from those of the habitants (xxx, 297). Where Beaumanoir overflows with metropolitan luxuries, the warehouse of Philibert (the building that bears the golden dog) contains the staples that form the wealth of Canada: furs, corn, wool, flax, and timber (xiii, 114). If this staple economy indicates a kind of rugged virtue, so does the habitant distaste for the inflationary, abstract *assignats* or promissory notes as opposed to their 'natural' system of commodity barter (xxxvi, 363–4). Though the entire system of *assignats* proved a desperate, misguided measure, it is typical of Kirby to couch his disapproval in moral rather than economic terms. He views the system as another instance of Old France casting its shadow over the New. Even theological controversy – the debate over the rigorous Jansenist system of Roman Catholic devotional practice – appears as an Old World oppression of the new (xlix, 514–5).

Kirby's rigid geographical designation of virtue is consistent with his most Gothic characterization, that of La Corriveau, a sorceress and poisoner. Just as Hawthorne took his Chillingworth (*Scarlet letter*) from the London of the Overbury murder, so Kirby chooses to emphasize strongly the overseas origins of the witch's mother. This was a matter of historical fact, but the author spends three digressive chapters detailing the sins of a Paris steeped in witchery, poison, and diabolism. They conclude with La Corriveau's boast of her impeccable lineage: ' "I come of a race ancient and terrible as the Roman Caesars!" ' (xxxiv, 353). Thus the fall of Quebec – prophesied on the occasion of Philibert's murder – will result from the burden of metropolitan corruptions (represented by Bigot, Angélique, La Corriveau, Beaumanoir, and La Friponne) laid upon the virtuous colony (represented by the Philiberts). Theirs are the Christ-like simplicities of *habitant* life, which is why Philibert, shortly before his death, offers his daily blessing of a dinner for twelve of the poor (L, 518).

From all this, the author draws a somewhat surprising moral. At one point, Bigot and his gang ride into a crowd in a fashion recalling Monseigneur's running-down of a child in Dickens' *A tale of two cities*. In view of this and other incidents, one might expect the book to offer cautionary advice to the rulers of society, as happens in that novel. No doubt some sort of admonition – a revolution will break out if our élite do not mend their ways – could be inferred from *The golden dog*, but the author instead chooses to gather from his story a bouquet for loyalty.

Early in the story we are assured that no matter how heinous the crimes of Bigot and *La Friponne*, they at least avoid the treacheries of the crypto-revolutionaries of New England, 'the disaffected remnant of Cromwellian republicans ... whose hatred to [sic] the Crown ever outweighed their loyalty, and who kept up a traitorous correspondence ... with the Governors of New France' (XIV, 135). Despite the crimes and follies visited upon it by a sinful homeland, New France will not only remain loyal to her bad parent during the remaining years of her existence, but maintain a tenacious loyalty to Britain during the American Revolution and after (LV, 573–4). In view of the imperial-colonial politics in the story, the reader might expect to find there a call to revolt. Philibert's wish to repurchase his family's one-time estates in France might seem contradictory, in view of the man's victimization by metropolitan greed and arrogance (XLVI, 487). These matters are not given much play in the novel. Its moralistic handling of social questions assures that loyalty becomes an end in itself, a virtue elevated far above the muck of history, a goal to be sought despite any practical considerations.

Kirby's vision of One Canada may verge on the ridiculous; it certainly seems like after-dinner rhetoric to announce that our national character blends French 'gayety' with the 'grave' aspects of the English, or that anglophone and francophone literatures merged when General Wolfe 'floated down' the St Lawrence reciting Gray's 'Elegy.' Perhaps this is why he dropped both comments when abridging his novel, though Wolfe as a Canadian Orpheus merits preservation.[24] More important to the matter of national unity than these shared distinctions remains the characteristic of loyalty. Both Ranger John in *The U.E.* and the benign old soldier La Corne St Luc of *The golden dog* would agree on that (XXI, 208). From the welter of treasons, vices, betrayals, murders, seductions, and poisonings, out of this *grand guignol* of tempestuous women and daredevil men, out of this picture of a frontier society at war, a war mismanaged by the mother country, Kirby extracts a single moral lesson: the need for loyalty. As that virtue is *the* mark of English Canada, the enduring myth and tradition there, so it may now unfurl itself as the sign of French Canada as well. Kirby has shaped the elements in his novel toward that conclusion, and wrenched history that way too.

III

Beneath Kirby's New World gardens lies the framework of the covenantal theology that runs through so many writings by and about Loyalists. Be but loyal, the pact states, and the Lord will safeguard you in the garden granted in the new land. There exists a corollary to that reassurance: let the mother country but nourish that garden, and it will repay her with steadfast fidelity. Of course, *The golden dog* shows the rupture of the colonial covenant, but that was in another empire, and besides the society is dead. The whorish mother moves to a doom she richly deserves, bearing the love and goodwill of the daughter she has neglected. No firm grounds for proof exist, but a student may speculate just how covertly the novel represents the author's conviction that *his* mother country stood guilty of violating its part of the covenant. Modern times have shown us how endemic these fears are in colonial societies, whose élites are forever fearing themselves sold out to slick, corrupt, and forgetful metropolitan elements. Kirby need not be seen as a district commissioner out of Kipling (as in such stories as 'The enlightenments of Pagett, M.P.' and 'A conference of the powers'), a white Rhodesian, or an Algerian *pied noir* to admit of the possibility that just as Dickens wrote about the Faubourg Saint-Antoine as a warning to Mayfair, so Kirby may have had a thought or two about Great Britain in his treatment of Old Quebec.

A present-day critic laments that the 'development of anything native in Canadian romance was probably hindered by this example given by Kirby of ready success with European models,' such as Scott and Dumas père.[25] But does not Kirby's novel demonstrate that a Loyalist sensibility has attained the strength and daring to impose its own imaginative version of Canada upon a culture quite remote from it in actual fact? Major Richardson's garrison, as we shall soon see, huddles fearfully in the wilderness. Kirby's garden resembles a jungle in its voracious, assimilative drives.

Kirby's vision of imperial / Loyalist citizenship strikes a modern reader as both narrow and ruthless. Intent on binding all Canada in its orbit, reaching out in space to knot a rope around Riel's neck and in time to graft French Canada's roots onto its own, that vision seeks a unity at all costs. The world must be a fearsome place indeed to demand that kind of stance. Just how terrible that world can be will become clear in the study of John Richardson.

3 Major John Richardson: The Loyalist in Disguise

To turn from Kirby to Richardson is to encounter many of Loyalism's preoccupations and dilemmas in a displaced and disguised form. Earlier, I described his work as midnight to Kirby's noon, though the two authors do not deal explicitly with the same matter. The same questions are there, however. There is the tension between social restraint (the garrison) and instinctual freedom (the wilderness). There is a political dilemma akin to the psychological one: that of the reconciliation of liberty and innovation with order and tradition. The Loyalists came down firmly on the side of the latter. Therein lay their rationale for denying the American Revolution and loathing its fruits. Now the so-called garrison mentality did not originate in the Loyalist experience, and the writings of Mrs Moodie demonstrate that Loyalist ties and associations are not necessary to maintain that cast of mind. What the writings of Richardson show is the extent to which a preoccupation over such matters as the conflict between liberty and order can be embodied within the forms of imaginative literature. To study Richardson is to realize how those questions cast themselves repeatedly before the Canadian writer.

Richardson's novels are not political allegories. His characters, overwhelmed by the wilderness's invitation to lawlessness, are not models of Loyalist subjects swept away by the forces of the Revolution. Yet the novels do lead the reader to speculate on the consequences of certain cultural and political attitudes. They mirror in a nightmarish manner concerns that are treated in a modulated, 'civilized' form in other writers. Richardson's canon lets the reader view the extremes of fear, the profound sense of the lawless and uncontrolled nature of the universe that can compel man to erect a social order that stresses civility, decorum and deference. That kind of fear prevents any sort of easeful stance in this world, compelling the viewer to distance himself from a reality that cannot bear too direct a gaze.

Yet if a student of our literature were asked to come up with the names of some writers clearly marked by Loyalist ideas and associations, he would probably arrive at the name of Mordecai Richler before mentioning Major John Richardson (1796–1852). He is, after all, our certified madman: the novelist-as-duellist, the tamer of wild deer, someone regarded by the garrison at Kingston as a card-sharp, the watcher of the Upper Canadian bush as an arena of sex and violence.[1] He eventually made his native land too hot to hold him. Failing ludicrously at a pork-barrel job of supervising a police force along the Welland Canal (he attempted to turn those worthies into something like a crack hussar regiment), he then bilked the assembly of Upper Canada out of the sum they had voted him to produce a history of the war of 1812. The grant, he decided, had paid for the first volume; nothing more would be forthcoming unless Clio were primed with further cash. He saw the sales of his work, except for *Wacousta*, stay in the hundreds, a discouragement that prompted him to reverse the Loyalist paradigm and flee to New York. There he functioned as an impoverished hack who excised from his novel of 1812 any derogatory references to the one-time enemies who were now to be his public.[2] He died poor and wretched, finally selling the Newfoundland dog he could no longer afford to feed. He had been trying to market a sensational biography (we would now call it a spin-off) of the actress-courtesan Lola Montez.[3] To a modern critic, his masterpiece *Wacousta* (1832) remains remarkable chiefly for the 'resounding enthusiasm with which it exploits a seemingly universal inclination for depravity, perversity and bad taste.'[4]

All this scarcely fits the traditional image of the Loyalist. Here stands no upright figure who, through plain living and monarchist thinking, elevates his new-found land into a sanctuary for right conduct. Restraint, probity, self-effacement, devotion to British institutions at whatever cost: searching for these qualities in either Richardson's life or writings begets frustration. If he had left behind no other trace, the Mr Sapsea sort of gravestone he erected to his first wife would have stamped him as one of the more full-blown of romantic egoists, Tennyson's Ulysses gone a bit strange.[5] Yet his Loyalist ancestry was impeccable, even to the extent of acknowledging the red as well as the white side of the Loyalist crest, since his grandmother was an Ottawa.[6] He had served as a gentleman-volunteer alongside Brock and Tecumseh in 1812. He had suffered for this allegiance as a prisoner of war (after the defeat at the Thames) in Kentucky. He had attempted to build a literary career in Britain afterwards, but had come pelting back to his homeland in 1837 when the British connection appeared threatened. His first published work was a mercifully small epic (in Byronic *ottava rima*) on that Loyalist icon Tecumseh (1828). In 1843, when he turned his hand to running a newspaper, he gave it a title that summed up the Loyalist myth of Upper Canada with the brevity of an advertising slogan: *Canadian Loyalist and Spirit of 1812*. Surely any survey of the influence of Loyalism on our literature must include this man whose extremism renders him all the more significant. His writings preach from the house-tops the fears and obsessions others muttered only beneath their blankets.

In speaking of the cultural fear that permeates the work of Richardson, the critic must avoid ascribing it to neurotic or perverse sources. No excursions into psycho-history need be undertaken to explain his experience. The Loyalists of Upper Canada had lost an earlier war, either in person or by ancestral proxy. They remained in their new land vulnerable to the assaults of a proximate, aggressive, and potent foe, and they saw themselves afflicted with actual and potential traitors in their midst. Late and fake Loyalists waited only for the chance to join the invaders. Traitors lurk in the work of Kirby and, as we shall see, in subsequent fiction. The savage, raid-and-destroy warfare along the shores of Lake Erie and in the Western and Niagara peninsulas, the grim repression of 'traitors,' these bear no small resemblance to the vicious theatres of civil war, Westchester County, New York, for example, during the American Revolution.[7] To those who fought like Richardson with the Right Division in the Western Peninsula, the savageries of frontier warfare had ended in bitter and humiliating defeat, the widespread destruction of a barely tamed countryside, and final imprisonment.

A recent writer suggests that some Canadian critics have Americanized Richardson (he attempted, after all, to do this himself). They view *Wacousta* through the Gothic glass of American literature instead of noting the debt it owes to Elizabethan revenge tragedy and the sentimental novel.[8] The question of literary sources is always important, yet even the most imaginative of writers owe something to life as well as to books. The savagery of the Richardsonian view may have as much to do with dead and despoiled Upper Canadians as with Jacobean playwrights and American Gothicists. That war of alarms, excursions, and defeats produced a literary sensibility humming with a sense of the anarchy of existence. In Richardson's world, horror has to be viewed with detachment if sanity is to last. We have a body of fiction which, rightly read by right-thinking folk, justifies their appetite for a rigid and dense social fabric.

I

Arguably the most popular of English Canadian novels in terms of its endurance over the decades, *Wacousta* went through six editions in its first eight years and was reprinted three more times during the century. It appeared again in 1806, and in 1903 it came out in a deluxe illustrated edition (C.W. Jefferys, of course). Finally, 1967 saw an abridged edition appear in the New Canadian Library series.[9] A dramatization of it by James Reaney appeared in 1978, and the novel was famous enough in its time to have been turned by one R. Jones into a melodrama. That version survives through a copy left behind by a touring actor after his company had played London, Ontario, in the 1850s.[10] No need for the road-show writer to have played up the novel's melodramatic aspects to satisfy the demands of the stage. The sheer volume of raw heads and bloody bones strewn across the pages were actually diminished onstage. Nor could the dramatist stomach the deaths of the most innocent of the characters; he let all of the De Haldimar children live.

That early stage adaptation's crudeness shows the formal sophistication of the novel, throwing into relief the complex nature of the original's time sequence. The novel initially presents events in a mysterious fashion and saves explanation of them for later chapters.[11] Though from one viewpoint this seems no more than a suspense-creating mechanism common to pot-boilers, that explanation does not convey the whole truth. For the novel is a powerfully integrated work; the world it envisions is composed of mysterious events reconstructed only with difficulty. This will be discussed more fully later; for the present, remember only that this narrative device, formulaic in appearance, also functions as a message of some significance.

Like so many later Canadian novelists, Richardson became a man of one book. He packed into this one all the themes and motifs that would appear fragmentarily in later productions. Thus, *Wacousta* presents the reader with a dense chain of circumstances convincing us that the necessities of the story decree that the children must die. In examining that density, we come to a fuller understanding of Richardson's vision and the despair it conveys about the resources of civilization.

II

In his *Patterns of isolation*, John Moss observes the polymorphous / perverse aspects of the novel's sexuality: the beautiful men admiring each other rather than women, the women who in their turn display a greater interest in their own sex than in the other, the females who pair with brutal dominators, and finally the strong sexual feelings surrounding brother / sister relationships. Moss's *Sex and violence in the Canadian novel* enters into greater detail on this subject, discovering that in *Wacousta* there is more to sex than sex itself. The 'sexual conundrum,' the triangle that we often encounter, defines an 'ideal condition of unity or completion, while showing it to be practically impossible or possible only on an arcane or esoteric level.'[12] What other meanings emerge from the sexuality in *Wacousta*?

If an erotic interest in members of one's own sex or family holds some connection with a habit of narcissism, then this mirror-gazing aspect of our sexuality pervades the novel. How clotted the story is with relatives, look-alikes, and namesakes! First, observe the De Haldimars, the sole survivor of whom marries a cousin. The De Haldimar girl attracts Wacousta's attentions not only for vengeance' sake. Her close resemblance to the mother whose name she bears interests him most of all. Secondly, recall Wacousta, who takes as his concubine the wife of his dead nephew. Both share the name of Reginald Morton. Finally, when the lover (who for some unaccountable reason is not a close relative) of young Clara mourns her loss, he is struck by her resemblance to her brother, whom he also deeply admired.

Coupled with this theme of mirror gazing is that of disguise or pseudonymity. Masking, considered from the standards of realist fiction, reaches operatic extremes. For 'opera,' one should perhaps read 'minstrel-show,' as when Wacousta appears before the British garrison in black-face, decked in a coffee-boy's turban.[13] The two Reginald Mortons appear disguised and pseudonymously, and the Wacousta Morton is also known as the fleur-de-lis warrior. Cooper's Natty Bumppo bore a string of names (Deerslayer, Hawkeye, Leather-stocking), but these were nicknames, not devices for concealment. The non-Wacousta Morton travels under the alias of Frank Halloway, since he is a gentleman now serving in the ranks in an attempt to evade his past. The officers of the garrison at Fort Detroit disguise themselves when in enemy country, a practice so commonplace that Colonel De Haldimar can spurn rather self-righteously Pontiac's denunciations of British espionage, In this book, two officers swanning about enemy country in disguise simply is not spying. The novel's 'fifth business,' an Indian woman whose love for the hero is exploited by the whites, appears as a warrior as often as she wears normal dress, while the carnival aspect of things gets truly enlivened by a young chieftain's masquerade as a beaver.

Here is a pervasive atmosphere of dubious and mistaken identities. Individuals either flow into each other or transform themselves with frightening ease into self-effigies, in the manner of myths and legends, red and white. Think of the procession of animist religions with their totems and metamorphoses, and then of a span of western literature running from Ovid to Kafka. The slipperiness of individual identity has become a modernist cliché, and I dread shunting *Wacousta* along a 'pre-modernist' track. Still, among all the signs of civilization's degeneration in the wilderness, none remain more apparent than the ease with which social and sexual identity reduce themselves to an affair of masks and postures. Once again, I stress that one must avoid a glib modernization of the novel, for Richardson's sense of civilization's vulnerability never becomes sufficiently rationalized to be extended consistently over every aspect of the novel.

To draw a comparison, enough of mind exists in Joseph Conrad's *Heart of darkness* to show that Marlow as well as Kurtz is threatened by the mindlessness of the river journey. Marlow must come up with a propaganda of the deed in which his concern for the unshakeable details of professional competence carries him through the threatened breakdown. This enables him finally to lie like a gentleman and thus sustain the illusions on which civilization rests. Richardson remains in his mind a conservative humanist rather than a modernist. His culturally degenerative disease attains epidemic, but never universal range. Colonel De Haldimar's civilized barbarity does him in no less than Wacousta's savagery condemns him, but two of the young, scarred lives remain. (It is significant, however, that in his sequel to *Wacousta*, *The Canadian brothers*, Richardson can only send the two off to the West Indies in a few paragraphs and have a hurricane dispose of them there.) Though the Indians massacre their enemies in lurid style, and the author bestows infernal epithets on them, the redcoats are not seen to carry out similar atrocities. They kill in a 'legal' fashion, and the author is not at all ironic about this. Even when, in later novels, the author comes to deal with killers, rapists, and cannibals on the order of Desborough and Westbrook, they remain horrifying examples of self-willed degeneration, ghoulish monsters who, however powerful, exert no appeal over the younger heroes.[14] Westbrook must be killed by a wolf who has taken to nursing his son, so removed is he from humanity and nature alike. Thus Richardson's villains are exactly that, rather than compelling anti-heroes.

The wolf-men, Desborough and Westbrook, remind us that the wilderness in which they exist bears a complementary rather than an originative relationship to their wickedness. They do not suddenly go native when exposed to the bush; they flee there because they have already become savage. Wacousta strives for a Byronic, melancholy grandeur during his lengthy flashback confession to Clara. Like any romantic worth his salt, he bases his story on a Miltonic myth: the paradise lost was the Edenic setting in which he first encountered Clara's mother. Her father, a rebel proscribed after the 1715 uprising, built a sexless paradise for them in which pastoral elegance blended both a library and a pet stag (Richardson in real life had to make do with a pet deer). Swept by bursts of emotion during his lengthy narrative extending over four chapters, Morton / Wacousta demonstrates that even the wilderness has not extinguished the remains of the man of feeling.

This remnant from a sentimental novel reminds us that we cannot consistently view Richardson's wilderness in stark opposition to the garrison. We are given imaginative bursts of terror which the resources of civilization seek to soften and explain. Yet this sense of cosmic terror comes through recurrent symbolic and narrative motifs, rather than through overt discourse. It is as much a matter of what the novel shows as it is of what the novel says. The sexless paradise is doomed; the evil underside of the garrison's values looms no larger than the wilderness's sympathetic response to the evil, yet some moral come-uppance remains. As the killing of Westbrook by the wolf indicates, even the bush has its limits.

If the dichotomies between bush and fort are not as radical as they first appear, what mark of his awareness of this does the author provide? Margot Northey wrote of the symbolic aspects of the bridge in *Wacousta* where so much of the action takes place. Here forest and fortress meet.[15] The bridge forms an enduring link (it is still there for the sequel, half a century later) between the two polarities. It serves as the avenue on which civilized man ventures out into a darkness which he assumes exists only out there, rather than within himself as well. In fact, the colonel's judicial murder of Frank Halloway happens on the bridge; the evil we see there owes nothing to the wilderness.

The moral complexities of the Richardsonian universe can be best glimpsed in a moment from *The Canadian brothers*, in which an Arcadian picnic of officers and their ladies concludes with one of the men bitten by a rattlesnake.[16] He is saved from death by a woman whose skills at handling snakebite make her seem 'a vampire and sorceress,' and she goes on to darker deeds.[17] In a part of the forest removed from this scene, the brute Desborough sits gnawing on a human arm he has cured and smoked. Can we think of these people as points along a line, or perhaps as figures standing along the bridge that links garrison with bush? The officers rest at one end, Desborough at the other. Between them stands the sorceress, practising her black arts with ease in the garrison society. Nowhere can the reader find a firm boundary; characters switch identities to suit their goals or pass easily from one realm to another.[18] All this makes the universe a haven of chaos and terror. The man of imagination responds to it by fixing what he must see into an aesthetic, distancing composition.

Richardson's regard for the picturesque carries a moral implication beyond that of a connoisseur's stance: the picturesque serves as a way of composing oneself in the face of bewildering or terrifying events. Consider the role it plays in Richardson's characteristic modes of perception. It is there in his first novel, *Écarté* (1829), where the author adopts a genre-painter's view of a slapstick tussle aboard a channel ferry: 'a scene which would not have disgraced the pencil of a Hogarth.'[19] One of the opening scenes in *Wacousta* is termed 'picturesque,' and the Hogarthian allusion recurs in his fiction, applied this time to a moment of comic horror that is termed a scene 'for some American Hogarth.'[20] Even the grim Westbrook, at the age of forty-five married to his seventh wife, manages to build a cabin in the bush which 'commanded a highly romantic aspect [of the Thames].'[21]

The author's historical writing also shows his painterly ways of observation: during the departure of a mixed expeditionary force from Fort Sandwich in 1812, the movement of the British regulars and the Indians over the ice 'gave an air of romantic grandeur to the scene,' while the burial of a chief's son creates 'a wild and romantic picture, in which melancholy grandeur shone principally conspicuous.'[22] Our visual knowledge of the years of Loyalist Upper Canada owes a great deal to the draughting skills of the British officers who sojourned here, and in Richardson, the gentleman volunteer, we find that skill alive in words.[23] In the manner of Paul Kane's paintings, the lineaments of the Indians are outlined in a classical terminology stressing the grandeur of their appealing postures, their 'true Grecian style of beauty.' Richardson goes on to show that these aesthetic stances involve moral considerations when he declares that 'so completely ... had my imagination been acted upon by the picturesque costumes of the men and women ... that I felt, that if I could always see them as presented to my observation, I would willingly pass the remainder of my days among them – a son of nature and subject only to nature's laws.'[24] The genre scenes, the vistas of romantic grandeur, convey the author's attempts at what Keats called 'stationing' when he admired it in Milton. A small but important detail of this skill at creating significant background occurs in *Wacousta*, where the room of Clara and Madeline De Haldimar at Fort Mackinac holds a collection of New World flora and fauna combined with Old World artefacts, a mark of their attempt to blend both places and live, as it were, on the bridge (chap. xix). Even when, at the end of his life, Richardson penned a pornographic romance about the Crusades, *The monk knight of St. John* (1850), he displayed an almost Spenserian power to describe erotic, violent encounters within carefully evoked settings that complement the actions and freeze them into a series of tableaux.[25]

Ultimately, man's hope for sanity in a world so beset with violence and confusion, a world where nature's serenity ceaselessly mocks man's disturbance, lies in his adoption of a beholder's stance.[26] This imaginative moral gesture lets the observer view with some understanding events and forces that can never be fully sounded by him. Recall again the narrative technique of *Wacousta*, and the way in which sections of the work open with mysterious occurrences which following chapters then strive to explain. Wacousta's flashback to his days as Reginald Morton offers an individual instance of what is a larger device of explanatory recollection in the novel. This technique defines the nature of the work's imaginative / moral stance. Experience remains discontinuous and inexplicable until the beholder has distanced himself from what he has seen. He can then fit it into some larger associative pattern, historical or symbolic.

Because Richardson's work is so frequently bad, because he so exuberantly breaks every canon of taste, critics have allowed persistent motifs in his fiction to go unremarked, as if they were only the formulaic devices of an unreflective imagination. Let me stress the qualifier, only. There are things to be learned even from so flawed a writer as Richardson: shoddy practices with grander implications. In the light of his concern with views and viewers, for example, one speculates on the significance of the voyeurism that so marks his narratives. The events in *Wacousta* must form our literature's most extensive peep-show. Characters are forever being peered at by others, and part of Wacousta's power lies in a talent for staring disconcertingly through windows. We have noticed the incidence of spying and masking in the novel, as well as its preoccupation with mistaken identity and concealment. If ambush served as the principal tactic of frontier warfare, then that very real aspect of the life he portrayed served Richardson's narrative habits well, adding another dimension to his motif of the unseen watcher. His two Fort Dearborn novels, *Hardscrabble* and *Wau-nan-gee*, take place within garrisons first unsuspecting of and then terrorized by their enemy's power to observe them from concealment. Lovers are caught nearly *in flagrante delicto* in *Écarté*, and one of the heroes in *The Canadian brothers* beholds in secret a father-daughter encounter with distinct sexual overtones. Loving couples are observed at play more than once in *The monk knight*, where one figure even enjoys fantasizing about a friend's embrace of the daydreamer's wife. Westbrook in his novel not only watches the lovers but later rapes the woman while forcing her lover to watch. Indeed, *Westbrook* offers an even more vivid indication of the author's interest in such matters: his memoirs, *Eight years in Canada*, tell of a low hotel in Brockville with room partitions rickety enough to see through. In his novel, the heroine stays at that hotel, where the villain observes her while she undresses.[27]

At this point, the reader may wish to account for this obsession by invoking whatever similar pathology motivates Richardson's interest in cannibalism and rape.[28] Yet voyeurism denotes terror as well as interest on the part of the peeper. It demonstrates not only a wish to participate in the act but a fear of the act itself, a fear of its seeming violence and brutality. Voyeurism remains a mode of establishing distance, a method of detachment. Thus when we examine that most erotic of Richardson's works, *The monk knight*, we find a paradox. The work frequently rhapsodizes about sex, even to the extent of excusing female homosexual contact on the grounds that 'should not one woman love as passionately as a man, what God made so perfect in another' (62). Yet, in the book sex intertwines with violence, deception, bondage, cannibalism, and burial alive. Could not the voyeuristic aspect of the Richardsonian stance be simply another instance of his attempted detachment from the horrors and confusions of an intractable universe? The observer watches events, though not primarily to participate imaginatively in what he sees (a pleasant side-effect), but to place it in some kind of perspective that will remove him from its terror. Richardson remains a humanist rather than a modernist because he continues to believe that terror is observed by gazing upon a tableau, rather than into a mirror.

This detachment occurs in other, less vivid ways, as in Richardson's repeated laments for a lost time of happiness and spontaneity. This strain runs through his writing, from the Eden of Reginald Morton and Clara Beverley's meeting place in *Wacousta* to the strident assertions of a lost emotional and sexual paradise in *The monk knight*.[29] While this sense of loss occurs in more groups than Loyalists alone, it strengthens in a small way my conviction that Richardson, for all his personal and fictional oddities, ought to be viewed within a broad framework of Loyalist outlooks. He belongs there because he reveals an underside of a phenomenon that is publicly confident and decorous. That confidence could stem from a willed superiority to the wilderness, a space which in fact presents considerable grounds for cultural despair. The place on which he stands remains shaky, shakier still those lost paradises in which a steadier existence seemed possible. The first Upper Canadian writer to reverence the figure of Tecumseh, Richardson began a process that would conclude with the chief's apotheosis in the drama of Charles Mair. But beyond the conventionalities of Richardson's verse lies an imaginativeness as a fiction writer that places him, for all his cultivation, gallantry, and certainty as to the rightness of his cause, upon a bridge. That bridge, like Satan's in *Paradise lost*, marks the bond between this world and hell.

III

Can Richardson and Kirby appear as a pair of complementary contrarieties, one of them the children on the old-fashioned weather-box, the other the old witch? Both deal with the means by which a culture comes to terms with the fact of violence. Kirby adopts the course which historically most cultures have followed; violence occurs within a highly ritualized and moral context ultimately sanctioning the society's participation. Skirmishes are won, murderers are scorned and punished, the guilty suffer pangs. In a word, the whole spectacle, however sanguinary and wasteful, *means* something. The other alternative, that of the night-world, appeals to Richardson. His is the fashion in which cultures mythically, rather than historically, handle violence. As in folklore, it does not intrude upon life but remains one of its conditions. I am thinking of the world of Grimms' Fairy Tales, where giants bite off heads while kings chop them off. No social grouping claims a monopoly over violence, since young giant-killers have as sure a right as kings to decapitate their enemies. Everyone is afraid, no one suffers guilt. Why should anyone feel guilty about bundling up against the cold?

The two authors together present a panorama of the way in which a culture hurled into existence by an act of war and sustained by further combat comes to view the nature of its heritage. For Kirby, the heritage implies a covenant, a providential contract through which conflicting claims and obligations are reconciled. To Richardson, the world offers no such plan by which virtue might be exercised and rewarded. One simply soldiers on.

Of course, even that exercise bears its complexities, as the next chapter will show. Since soldiers lose as well as win battles, how shall their defeat be made glorious? The battleground, however, has been laid out and reconnoitered by Kirby and Richardson.

4 Charles Mair, Tecumseh, and the Lost Garden

I

Does the Loyalist hero exist? Most of the works this study examines celebrate a collectivity, the group's endurance and grit. If textbook illustrations, speeches, and monuments are any guide, then Upper Canada's hero is Brock, the sacrificial soldier.

Where imaginative literature is concerned, however, one sustained effort exists where the entire work is built around the figure of a single man who embodies the classic Loyalist dilemmas. Charles Mair (1838–1927) drew the tragic portrait of the Loyalist warrior in his 1886 drama, *Tecumseh*. *Dreamland and other poems* (1868), a set of romantic nature lyrics, earned Mair the title of 'the Canadian Keats,' and *Tecumseh* in its way resembles another Keatsian enterprise. The hero-as-loser, whose life derives its fullest resonance from the manner of his leaving it, preoccupies Mair as it did Keats in *Hyperion*. Tecumseh is no Titan; no one could ever confuse Mair's blank verse with the Miltonic stateliness of Keats' epic fragment. Both works derive from a similar cultural enterprise: accounting for decline and fall by placing it within a scheme of ultimate optimism. Keats' Titan yields gracefully to Apollo, and Tecumseh's nobility instils a sense of heroism and constancy in the Upper Canada he helps to save. The blood of martyrs is the seed of the church.

We have here a widespread romantic and post-Christian strategy, the substitution of a secular myth of death and resurrection to fill the vacuum left by the disappearance of the supernatural one. In order to create an optimistic structure of meaning that will transform defeat into triumph, Mair ignores any unsettling insinuations provided by his historical material. Kirby's *The golden dog*, as we have seen, cobbled a message of fidelity out of the depiction of a colonial relationship marked by neglect and exploitation. Mair's idealized hero somehow stands for a set of happy resolutions to the intractable problems of a death occasioned by abandonment and neglect. What forces made this victimized defender of Upper Canada an icon of Loyalism? The beginnings of an answer to that question can be found in an examination of the historical Tecumseh. Later, we can encounter the figure Mair made of him.

Tecumseh so captured the imagination of his destroyers that Hoosiers once thought seriously of naming their state capital after him.[1] Could this be another instance of what one could call the Walter Scott syndrome, whereby the conquering, modernizing culture dons the kilts of whatever group it has exterminated and goes on to celebrate the charming fossil in story and song? The unsettling implications of the Shawnee chieftain's struggle and defeat still cannot be comfortably accepted, which is why a 1974 outdoor drama concludes with the soothing syrup that Tecumseh's failure inspires all Indians with 'the living belief that some day and some way, there will be a better time.'[2]

Surely they order these matters differently in Upper Canada. For Tecumseh remained its strongest ally in the second Loyalist war. In view of the great chief's career, that red hand clutching a tomahawk on the UEL crest seems no sentimental allusion to a fabled past. Tecumseh proved a very important figure in the saving of Upper Canada; if such things as Loyalist paragons exist, then he, no less than Brock, is one of them. Indeed, in terms of sustained creative interest, the Shawnee has occupied a larger role in the imaginations of artists and poets than Brock. We find works on Tecumseh ranging in publication dates from 1828 to 1976, from Major John Richardson's epic to Don Gutteridge's sequence of poems. Though Mair's drama on the subject remains the most ambitious, sustained and best-remembered attempt to come to grips with the tragic career of the Indian leader, Upper Canada really deals with the man no better and no less evasively than its southern cousins. The evasiveness is of a different sort but, as I intend to demonstrate, it exists. The aspect of Tecumseh's career that Mair glosses over reveals much about the Loyalist imagination.

That career takes on a new significance in light of what we know about other anti-imperialist leaders and their role in a colonial dynamic. Tecumseh was the last of the great fighters that the natives of the eastern half of the continent put up against white occupation of their lands. He stands in a line that includes King Philip and Pontiac. One of Tecumseh's principal enemies, who rode to the White House on his skill in provoking a battle with Tecumseh's forces during their leader's absence, wrote officially that 'if it were not for the vicinity of the United States, Tecumseh, would, perhaps, be the founder of an empire that would rival in glory Mexico or Peru.' Colonial generals enjoy exaggerating the strength and ruthlessness of the opponents they plan to wipe out, but more than one white enemy was struck by the chief's personal and public graces.[3]

Our present-day interest extends beyond the consideration of his qualities as a war leader and tireless organizer. The nature of his political movement and his complex relationship with the white powers he came up against also compel our attention.[4] Tecumseh's leadership did not exist within a cultural vacuum; it took considerable strength from the primitivist, puritan ideology of his brother, Tenskwatawa or the Prophet. Nineteenth-century historians – Charles Mair was to follow their approach in his play – despised the religious showman who dazzled his followers with solar eclipses he had learned to predict from the enemy's almanacs and then terrified them with his penchant for sniffing out 'witches' who might serve as potential dissidents. We can no longer view the Prophet as Hyde and his brother as Jekyll. Of course, the Prophet and his forces fled from the scene of Tippecanoe, but it is not as a war leader that he throws light on Tecumseh. Recall the significance of the role played by primitivist religious movements in colonial struggles: Mahdism in the Sudan and the witch-cult in the newly conquered Matabeleland of 1896 offer two examples. The phenomenon of Wahabism in what is now Saudi Arabia provided the strength to pull that region out of the system of Hashemite puppet kings the British Colonial Office had prepared for it in 1919. The term 'mad mullah' pops up frequently enough in anecdotal memoirs of British colonial officers to make us aware of this dimension to native resistance.

Thus the Prophet's call for abstention from alcohol, the cultivation of indigenous foodstuffs, and the avoidance of contact with whites no longer seems a desire for a set of whimsical blue laws but the kind of practical, purgative, and self-defining measures necessary for tribal resistance to a strong invader. To Tecumseh's message of red solidarity and tribal confederation for purposes of resistance, the Prophet added a cult reaffirming the values of the resistance. And the witch-hunt provided the revolutionary instrument of terror, the constant surveillance and ruthless discipline necessary for the success of any resistance movement. Tecumseh's agile use of the strengths of his brother to grant his movement an extraterritorial dimension marks his skill as a resistance leader.

A similar sophistication characterizes his dealings with whites, enemies and allies alike; Tecumseh demonstrated a knack for playing off one set against another rather than locking himself into a short-sighted hostility to all. Though he had good reason to remember that the British were quite prepared to abandon their Indian allies in the interests of maintaining an uneasy peace with the Americans, he also knew better than to let that grudge stand in the way of securing whatever Britain could give.[5] After his greatest error – his absence from Tippecanoe, which tempted his brother to seek martial as well as necromantic glory – Tecumseh sought to take advantage of the impending war between Britain and her former colonies. He urged the British to adopt a bellicose policy, promising them his aid in return for their backing of his claims at the peace table.[6] He then played the British card – none other was left – and lost. His cause perished with him. The treaty commissioners that Britain had sent to Ghent cried that 'It is utterly inconsistent with ... [Great Britain's] practice and her principles ever to abandon in her negotiations for peace those who have co-operated with her in war.'[7] Yet that is exactly what happened.

How did this beggared and betrayed native resistance leader ever get placed in the Loyalist collection of tame Indians? What traits in him and in Loyalist mythology itself made him appear along with Brock in a Canadian Heroes series of popular biography? Why should the meeting between Tecumseh and Brock have produced one of C.W. Jefferys' most dramatic historical vignettes?[8]

II

He defended Upper Canada against an American invasion. His compelling personality, his uniqueness as an Indian leader, the aura of a lost cause made him a subject impossible for any romantic culture to ignore. To expand upon these explains why he attracted the attention of Richardson, Mair, and a host of other Loyalist writers and historians. It also reveals those aspects of Tecumseh and his struggle which any Loyalist affirmation of him needed to underplay, alter, or ignore.

Tecumseh's role in the defence of Upper Canada was decisive, noble, and sacrificial. Decisive: the Indian alliance gave to General Brock the edge his forward policy needed. To rally a wavering populace required more than the audacious deployment of his tiny force of regulars, the mustering of the militia, and the use of the resources of government to cow the disaffected. A speedy and decisive victory was needed; the surest way to compensate for the overwhelming superiority of the American forces at and about Detroit lay in raising the spectre of the savage frontier warfare that British, Loyalists, and Indians had waged so effectively in 1776. No one can say if pictures of

Wyoming and Cherry Valley flashed through the mind of General Hull at Detroit, but Brock's message to him, with its pained admission that he could not guarantee being able to bridle his savage allies once their blood was up, offered at least a nudge in that imaginative direction. The Hull who foundered so precipitately was a frightened and confused general. Tecumseh's forces, by their very existence, helped keep him that way. Their successful harassment of Hull's lines of communication added substance to the terror they aroused.[9] Had Tecumseh helped his white allies no more than that, he would still have merited their deep gratitude.

Noble: even so confident a partisan as Major Richardson felt compelled to devote a portion of *The Canadian brothers* to a defence of British unwillingness to fight a whites-only war. Yet, as no historian or writer has ever failed to mention, Tecumseh not only loathed the practice of torturing captives and suppressed it in his own forces but on more than one occasion prevented the killing of prisoners. Once again, let Major Richardson's eyewitness accounts stand for many others, and observe there the frequent references to the chief's distinguished bearing, compelling oratory, and military dash.[10] Upon the death of Brock, he remains the sole heroic personage in the accounts, and Richardson, as has been noted, found him worthy of an epic. To later generations he became not only a good fighter to have had on one's side, but a gallant and humane ally as well.

Sacrificial: Tecumseh was to watch his and Brock's victory frittered away. A cease-fire (ordered by Governor Prevost in Montreal) gave the Americans time to reinforce their defences and build their fleet at Sackets Harbor. The death of Brock at Queenston Heights placed Henry Procter in command of regulars and militia. A number of frustrating investments and sieges – rather than lightning raids on American supply lines – wasted lives and lowered morale. Though Procter finally had no option but to retreat from the west once the battle of Put-in Bay – and the fleet that should have been burned while it lay a-building at Sackets Harbor – had given the enemy command of the lakes, Tecumseh found the withdrawal a hasty one. With difficulty he forced his allies to make a stand at Moraviantown, and even then Procter managed to leave his own men behind and scuttle with his baggage to Burlington Heights. At the last battle, Tecumseh inspired both his own and the white troops. Exhausted, they were soon broken. Only Tecumseh's desperate forces gave the Kentucky mounted riflemen any spirited resistance. Thrown away by inert strategies devised by inferiors, a Spartacus-like chieftain who personally heartened his own and his ally's forces until the very end, Tecumseh gained a mysterious grandeur in death. Its very circumstances were disputed (though a number of Americans claimed the honour of killing him, one carrying it as far as the vice-presidency) and his final resting place remains unknown.[11]

A more colourful conclusion to life can scarcely be imagined: the tall figure, a plume in his cap, rallied his troops with his remarkable voice until death and a mysterious resting-place claimed of him all that had been mortal. A matter for epic treatment, as Major Richardson saw, and in 1828 he published, under the pseudonym of An English Officer, *Tecumseh; or, the warrior of the west.* The rhyme scheme (in near *ottava rima*, the final alexandrine being omitted), with its comic, *Don Juan* associations, could not be better suited for reducing tragedy to bathos, yet the author sought 'to preserve the memory of one of the noblest and most gallant spirits that ever tenanted the breast of man.'[12] This imaginative preservation takes place amid what with hindsight we recognize as a familiar Richardsonian environment: an eroticized wilderness in which hellish savageries take place (canto 2: stanzas 6, 10); a Miltonic, melodramatic setting of 'colossal grandeur' (1: 45), peopled with horrific monsters (2: 43); a heroic protagonist possessed of an uncannily powerful voice (1: 22–3) and knotted with hatred for his unjust foes (1: 40–1). These previews of *Wacousta* need not concern us as much as the specifically nationalist thrust that Richardson gives his hero's energies: 'And swore to fall, or set his country free' (1: 35). During a midnight meditation before his last fight, Tecumseh envisions the long roll of Indian losses in the struggle with the whites. It is this, rather than the loss of his son (a mythical child upon whom Richardson bestows the Cooperish name of Uncas), which most distresses him. His deepest despair stems from his knowledge that he cannot preserve his people from defeat and extinction on the morrow. Yet this nationalist leader, 'the high, the noble, the generous, the unfortunate Tecumseh' (115), dies filled with hatred for his foes (4: 51). Here is no nationalist St Isaac Brock, a Christian knight to be prayed into his monument, but the savage vengeance-seeker Richardson would later immortalize in Reginald Morton/Wacousta. Quite properly, Richardson cannot forbear a Byronic allusion (4: 33), for it is from this mould rather than a Christian one that his hero springs. What the epic shows is that this figure – 'Fired with much spoil, and drunk with human gore' (4: 48) – as a monument to the spirit of national resistance remains a far cry from the Loyalist saint evoked in later textbooks and popular biographies.

Yet the need existed for a hero at once more romantic than the colourless Brock, but softened enough to remain appealing to a respectable audience. Upper Canada also required a Tecumseh whose sacrifice, however noble personally, did not appear futile and meaningless, the pathetic upshot of his role in imperial games whose scope lay beyond the bush of British North America. Charles Mair's *Tecumseh* was to fill that need, and a sense of the strength of those drives can be gained by observing the sentimentalization of Tecumseh that happened on the heels of Mair's play.[13] A year after it came Sarah Ann Curzon's verse drama on Laura Secord. The authoress had in vain asked Mair to help in defraying the expenses of publication, and her boldness in the matter was probably heightened by the linkage of her heroine to his hero.[14] In the 'Memoir of Mrs Secord' introducing the drama, Mrs Curzon invented out of whole cloth a tradition that Tecumseh had been in love with Laura's daughter Mary. The belief that, as a youth, Tecumseh grew romantically interested in an Indiana farm girl, Rebecca Junkin (later Galloway), appears in one current, uncritical biography.[15] Her transplantation to Upper Canada and the family of one of the best-known Loyalists bears no authority beyond that of the need for a gentler, more localized Tecumseh. That same pious legend flourished after Mrs Curzon, for we find it again, half a century later, in a popular historical novel on *Laura the undaunted* (1930). And one would indeed expect to find it in a novel that is mostly a cavalcade of Loyalist legends, including the virtual reduction of Brock's forces at Queenston Heights to militia units.[16] Like the story contained in 'The Cherry Tree Carol,' the Tecumseh-Secord union provides a charming addition to sacred history. It also demonstrates that the figure of Tecumseh has been sufficiently domesticated to support this sort of legend. For the process that accomplished this, we must now turn to Mair's drama.

III

Nearly sixty years separate Richardson's turgid cantos from Mair's five-act Shakespearian pastiche. If, as Michael Tait has pointed out, the play exhibits 'the utter lack of unity of action,' it may stem not only from a weakness in dramatic craft, but from the unruly nature of the historical material the author seeks to mould.[17] In addition, Mair seems determined to apply the idea of Loyalism to contemporary historical processes. At the time Mair sought to complete his play, the final act of a tragedy whose prologue he had helped stage was drawing to a close. Riel's impending execution obsessed Mair during the completion of a work he had been writing for five years; 16 November 1885 saw the hanging of the nationalist leader, mid-December the finish of *Tecumseh*.[18]

The provocative, fanatical, and less-than-noble role Mair assumed in the Red River uprising of 1870 remains the stuff of politics. Its import for this study lies in the fact that Mair chose to the end of his life to view the whole sorry business as a matter of loyalty and Loyalty. In such terms did he ennoble his anti-Métis activities, and his last word on the subject still viewed the Canadian annexationist minority as a group of heroic Loyalist settlers.[19] We need not concern ourselves with the mental gymnastics by which a group of Uitlanders came to see themselves as representing an authority so legitimate as to supersede all older and conflicting claims in the region. The importance of the annexation of the concept of Loyalty lies in the fact that the Protestant Ontario in which Mair and John Schultz preached a crusade of vengeance for the execution of Thomas Scott had for some time equated loyalty with the slogans of the Loyal Orange Order. Just as the post-1812 era of the Family Compact saw a concept of Loyalism expand to include participation in 1812, and later, 1837, so the imperialist nationalism of Canada First and even the throne-and-pulpit fulminations of Orangeism could all be grouped in a way that traced their mythic origins back to historical Loyalism itself.[20] Thus when Colonel George T. Denison blustered about mounting an insurrection should the government of Canada fail to pursue correct policies at Red River, he could appeal to an ahistorical, timeless Loyalty, as his Ulster cousins were later to do while preaching and arming for revolt in 1914.

Of course the coming death of Riel loomed over Mair during the completion of his play. He had warned Ottawa repeatedly of the conditions that would spark the North-West rebellion, and certainly had his doubts about the harsh sentence given Riel.[21] *Here*, in Windsor, was nearly completed a drama folding primitive hero and British general alike into a vision of one Canada; *there*, Regina, was nearly finished a judicial murder demonstrating to generations of Quebec nationalists their exclusion from that national vision. Riel was hanged, every dog in Quebec barked, and the drama – dedicated to 'The survivors of Canada First' when the inflexibility and divisiveness of their brand of national unity was becoming apparent – appeared to shouts of praise[22] What did it say?

It attempted to say a great deal, which returns us to the difficulties with unity of action. Its three story-lines include the career of Tecumseh from shortly before Tippecanoe to Moraviantown, the rallying and defence of Upper Canada as accomplished by Brock and a Loyalist *levée en masse*, and the romance between a white wanderer, Lefroy, and an Indian maiden, Iena. Irrelevant as this last complication may appear when placed against the historical panorama of the other story-lines, it holds considerable importance in locating the overall message of the play and the historical dilemmas it seeks to resolve.

As if his appearance carrying a rifle and examining a knot of wild flowers were insufficient to establish Lefroy's poetical character, he so personifies a romantic artistic stereotype in both manner and speech that an enemy soldier sword-fighting with him easily identifies him for what he is.[23] Lefroy is more important as poet than lover. While the business between him and Iena *is* irrelevant (except to show the strictness of the Prophet's laws against miscegenation), the poet's description of the west is not. As Tait notes, in a statement tying together the political with the poetical Mair, Lefroy's account of the prairies constitutes 'a first step in bringing the Canadian West under imaginative control.'[24] Within the play itself, the set-piece poem throws forward a vision of the Canadian landscape, immense and lonely, into which but one kind of man fits: 'the sunburnt savage free' (1: 2).

Lefroy's vision is irreconcilable with the historical business at hand. The same is true of his own doings, since he is nothing but trouble to the two heroes. His desire for Iena brings Tecumseh into conflict with his brother, while Brock is drawn into arguments about the nature of freedom and civility. Lefroy's outburst against the Americans (2: 4), warning them of a time when the poor will take their revenge upon the rich, was considered 'socialist' at the time of first publication.[25] It is no more so than the Magnificat. It is the debate between Lefroy and Brock (4: 6) that illuminates both in its content and context the problems with which the play deals.

Lefroy has seen beyond the romantic liberalism that prophesies an end to kings and gods. He knows that gold (that is, economic questions) produces tyranny's tightest stronghold. Gold must go before 'man can rise / Rightly self-made, to his high destiny.' Brock can only reply to this that what was good enough for his father was good enough for him. Like Ulysses in *Troilus and Cressida*, he points to a domino theory of social cohesion that King-Crown-Loyalty are an interwoven trinity, 'omitting these, man's government decays.' It is then, at Brock's request, that Lefroy delivers the play's best poetry in describing his prairie journeys with Tecumseh.

Since the debate has in fact become a cross-talk, let us pause here. The debate digresses from the central action: the grinding down of Tecumseh and his cause by rival imperialisms. Neither the dilemmas of modern liberalism nor the obstinacies of blind conservatism throw light upon the wrecking of Tecumseh and his cause. Instead, we retreat from the tensions raised by irrelevant political ideologies into aesthetic contemplation. Lefroy declaims upon the loveliness of the west as well as the competition for survival amid that solitude. From here, it is easy to remark on Tecumseh's prowess in the buffalo hunt. Brock wonders if Lefroy has not been dreaming all this. How right he is! The evocation of the west has topped a grand escape from the dilemmas posed by the action. The conclusion of the scene with Brock's praise of his ally and the statement that Tecumseh 'heaps / Such giant obligations on our heads / As will outweigh repayment' offers a neat, evasive, and historically quite accurate conclusion. Tecumseh has been lauded, and the primitive, natural world from which he draws his strength reverenced. Now the business of love and war can continue.

John Matthews has commented that the alliance between Brock and Tecumseh produces the ideal Canadian identity: loyalty and conservatism plus primitive ruggedness and virtue. Lefroy lurks in the background as a romantic dream.[26] The comment ignores the matter of the play's outcome. It ends with Tecumseh and Brock dead, Lefroy wandering off-stage with the corpse of his love who has sacrificed her life for his, and a sympathetic American general intoning a pious memorial for his dead foe. The wide, remote prairies seem a dream to the beleaguered defenders of Upper Canada. The questions of liberty and order – themselves a diversion from tragic contemplation – digress into a meditation upon an alien landscape. Thus finally can the problems of placing this collection of losers and martyrs within a pantheon for national identity be ignored.

To return to a previous point: an effort to reconcile a number of irreconcilable historical processes leads to the play's disunity. Tecumseh, the congenital Loyalist, in the depths of defeat at the hands of the Americans takes joy from the recollection that the British are his people's friends (3: 7). To them his fullest allegiance is given. This they repay with incompetent leadership that will abandon him and his cause. Lefroy seeks to reconcile the world of guns with that of flowers, the limitless west with the embattled east, and, in his pursuit of Iena, red with white. The upshot of it all is Iena's death and his own alienation. Brock perishes to take his place amid the constellations, but his concern for his Indian ally does not survive his end. The play offers a set of rather strange vindications of loyalty and Loyalism.

The Loyalist mythology knows no better encapsulation than occurs in the song of the York Volunteers (4: 3). In three eight-line verses, their metre that of 'Bonnie Dundee,' they warn that an enemy threatens to undo the work that made a forest into a 'redeemed' land. The sons must fight and if necessary die to defend it, but a united empire will assure the success of their cause. Colonel Denison thought it a patriotic rouser, commissioned a Mr Gledhill to set it to music, and 'For Canada Fight' was sung to a packed house at the Pavilion Music Hall in Toronto on 11 March 1886.[27] In fact, the play implies a darker vision of Loyalism than the Volunteers' hymn would suggest. Remember, the empire's narrow triumph accompanies the indigenous, red Loyalists' defeat through the efforts of imperial bunglers. We should recall how Kirby's *The golden dog* warns that metropolitan greed and decadence threaten the virtue and survival of the loyal New France. Mair's notes at the back of

Tecumseh, written (the preface informs us) to enlighten an ignorant mother country about various aspects of the drama, allude to a covenant: 'And Jonathan said to David. Go in peace, forasmuch as we have sworn both of us in the name of the Lord, saying, the Lord be between me and thee, and between my seed and thy seed forever' (1 Samuel, 20: 42).[28] Yet we find a Kirby-like uneasiness about the imperial understanding of the pact: 'With all her faults, Canada has ever been true to the high idea [of a united empire]. Even when the mother-country seemed ignobly to falter and fall away, she saw in it the indispensable safe-guard of our common interests, and with enlarged confidence in her own future, looks forward to its fulfilment still with abiding faith' (preface, p. 6).[29]

A number of devices in the play prevent *Tecumseh* from exploring the subversive implications of its hero's fate. The distractions posed by the other story-lines, the preoccupation with a detached, apotheosized Tecumseh rather than with a historical resistance leader (e.g., the downgrading of the Prophet into a fraudulent and sinister coward), the frequent employment of contrasting characters (Proctor [*sic*], the 'bad' English general, as opposed to Brock) turn collective issues into individual, moral ones. These submerge the implication that Loyalism is fast changing into an aspect of Canadian nationalism, since the necessary reciprocal imperial commitment is fading. Part of the hyperbolic and overwrought tone of Canada First may come as the result of trying to yoke together the forces of imperialism and nationalism. As the contradictions in *Tecumseh* indicate, these forces are experiencing a certain strain in their union.

Mair's Loyalist hero displays a Job-like persistence: 'Though he slay me, yet will I trust in Him.' From one viewpoint a tragic acceptance of insoluble contradictions, from another the play is a confused acquiescence, even to the point of defeat, in the dilemma posed by national versus colonial interests. This inability to resolve dilemmas inherent in the nature of Canadian experience itself we shall soon see as no minor aspect of Mair's writings.

IV

Mair's evasion of the logical consequences of Tecumseh's defeat remains the most significant of the Loyalist aspects of his drama, though the rest of his writings convey another theme we have encountered earlier. Mair proved a force in the Upper Canadianization of the west; his replication of the Loyalist theme of a paradise lost lies rooted in a spatial concept: the eminent rightness of Upper Canadian values turns the west into a garden for the taking. Settlements and agriculture – villages and gardens – are destined to supplant the nomadic and hunting culture now holding the land. As often happens, a deep regret for the liberties of the destroyed culture accompanies the hard-headed pragmatism that flattens it. Mair found in the new territories of west and north a paradise to be perpetually won and lost. Its very winning introduced the soulless modernization that was the stamp of the liberal and materialist culture of central Canada. Vacancy serves as the characteristic spatial form in the writings of Mair we next examine. Occupying this void puts the settler in a no-win situation: either he abandons the joyous, spontaneous aspects of his personality, or lets it flourish, but at a cost of anarchy and dissolution. The problem of environment seems central to Mair's writing, in that his derivative verse (he could as easily have been termed the Canadian Coleridge, Shelley, and Tennyson as the Canadian Keats) never appears quite rooted in a Canadian context. For example, the closest Mair could come to Canadianizing his Tennysonian echo, 'Summer,' was to cram the Loyalist pin-up of Laura Secord into its dream of fair women.[30]

'The legend of Chileeli,' a work published in 1885, shortly before *Tecumseh*, adds to our understanding of the contradictory aspects of Mair's political / poetical quest and to the split nature of his writings. In view of its author's career as poet and man of affairs, it appears as masked autobiography. The Keatsian, Tennysonian style of the poem and the stock romantic nature of its story of a troubled artist should not distract the reader from its personal implications. The poetical young Indian of the title turns himself into an efficient killer in order to win the approval of the father of his nameless beloved. He becomes absorbed enough in massacre and mutilation to notice no longer the natural beauties he passes on his raids. The girl disappears and is transformed into a bird. She then appears to Chileeli in a vision, scolding him for his loss of imaginative faith. Chileeli cannot deny the truth of the charges, and at the poem's end he disappears also. A man who passed his mature life in poetry, politics, and land speculation without achieving any remarkable success in any of them might well write such a poem about self-betrayal and the abandonment of spiritual goals for fleshly ones. But would he need to fill the poem with such an amount of vacancy? The maiden simply drifts into the forest, never to be seen again except as bird or vision; Chileeli slinks away, to be recalled only in the legend related by the poet. To its familiar theme has been added a passivity and emptiness denoting despair rather than tragic conflict.

To jump from here to the public letters that Mair sent back to Ontario during his first journey to the Red River in 1868–9 demonstrates how the blankness of 'Chileeli' reinforces certain themes in Mair's writing. The letters are exercises in the 'booming' of the 'New Canada.' They rhapsodize over the richness of the soil, the virtues of the climate, and the ease with which its present inhabitants can be fitted into the purposes of the colonization that must follow. The obtusely arrogant, Upper Canadian tone of the letters served to get their author horsewhipped by a lady he had insulted in one of them and made him the target of a satirical novel.[31] The letters also enabled him to play upon an image familiar in Loyalist writings: 'Before the settler stretches through immeasurable distance the large and livelier Canada – the path of empire and the garden of the world.' The land, a covenantal phrase asserts, 'drops fatness, as if in the fulfilment of prophecy; at once generous and abundant and more durable than its tiller.'[32] This garden, than which 'the world cannot offer a scene of superior promise, or of finer pastoral sweetness and content,' this 'haunt of the Indian, the bison and the antelope,' now awaits 'with majestic patience for the flocks and the fields, the schools, the churches, the Christian faith and love of freedom of the coming man.'[33]

We remain a way from Chileeli, but we can come closer in recounting Lefroy's prairie descriptions in *Tecumseh*:

> We left
> The silent forest, and day after day,
> Great prairies swept beyond our aching sight
> Into the measureless West; uncharted realms,
> Voiceless and calm, save when tempestuous wind
> Rolled the rank herbage into billows vast,
> And rushing tides which never found a shore.
> And tender clouds, and veils of morning mist,
> Cast flying shadows, chased by flying light,
> Into interminable wildernesses,
> Flushed with fresh blooms, deep perfumed by the rose,
> And murmurous with flower-fed bird and bee.
> The deep-grooved bison paths like furrows lay,
> Turned by the cloven hoofs of thundering herds
> Primeval, and still travelled as of yore.
> And gloomy valleys opened at our feet –
> Shagged with dusk cypresses and hoary pine;
> And sunless gorges, rummaged by the wolf,
> Which through long reaches of the prairie wound,
> Then melted slowly into upland vales,
> Lingering, far stetched among the spreading hills. (4: 6)

The poet evokes a vast emptiness; later, he will insert Tecumseh into it during a buffalo hunt. Here is the west of the Big Lonely – for the poet a world elsewhere, for the colonist an untended garden to be turned into the triumph of a prophecy.

'The legend of Chileeli,' with its betrayed promises, appears in the same volume with 'The last bison' (1890), a work ultimately deriving from Gray's 'The bard.' Here, the last buffalo speaks to the entranced poet about the coming dissolution of the culture that has destroyed him. In the same year as the poem, appeared Mair's article on 'The American bison,' lamenting that 'there is perhaps no fact in the natural history of America which brings such reproach on civilized man as the reckless and almost total destruction of the bison.'³⁴ Part of the betrayal and frustration in the struggle to be both lover and poet, warrior and visionary, that lie behind the blankness of 'Chileeli' can be located in the increasing sense of the destructive and irrevocable changes that had swept over the garden of 1869. Another vision has been betrayed, another visionary swept into the world of affairs.

After all, Mair's Tecumseh lies himself suspended between the lost tribal world, the Ohio valley homeland of his people, and the Upper Canadian and imperial realities that will willingly expend him in their fight. The confederation the chief creates can survive neither the shamanistic leadership of the Prophet nor the statesmanlike guidance of Tecumseh himself. Lefroy finds no happiness in either white or red worlds. Tecumseh's involvement with one imperial power hastens his destruction at the hands of the other. Adequately translated, these traps show up also as Loyalist dilemmas, problems of a remnant caught between the need to exploit and the wish to redeem an environment, conscious at once of imperial nurturing and imperial distractedness in which their needs could be absent-mindedly overlooked. The mind dizzys at the sight of these fissures, these cliffs of fall. Can heroic myths bridge them? The bridge in *Wacousta* witnessed both the horrors of savagery and the brutalities of civilized repression. Only a very heroic, detached, idealized figure – such as Mair's Tecumseh – can survive on that bridge.

Mair's last writing dealt with his journey to the Peace River country in 1899, where he helped negotiate the final treaties with the Indians and mixed-blood people living there. An old man's book, it is awash with nostalgia for a golden age whose destruction he was himself helping to bring about:

The writer ... can recall the time when to go to 'Peace River' seemed almost like going to another sphere, where, it was conjectured, life was lived very differently from that of civilized man ... [Its natives seemed] a very simple folk indeed, in whose language profanity was unknown, and who had no desire to leave their congenial solitudes for any other spot on earth: solitudes which so charmed the educated minds who brought the white man's religion, or traffic, to their doors that, like the Lotus-eaters, they, too, felt little craving to depart ...

Such was the state of society in that remote land in its golden age ...

We were now in close contact with the most innocently wild, secluded, and apparently happy state of things imaginable – a real Utopia, such as Sir Thomas More dreamt not of, being actually here, with no trace of abortive politics or irritating ordinance. Here was contentment in the savage wilderness – communion with Nature in all her unstained purity and beauty.[35]

With difficulty he covers his disappointment at the up-to-dateness of the inhabitants by invoking the benefits of progress (54–5, 117). Mair distances the hurt of watching the mixed-bloods drunkenly squandering the land scrip given them in exchange for their hunting rights by terming the scene 'worthy of an impressionist's pencil' (74). He notes as well the Richardsonian features of the place: a mad Iroquois who first murdered and ate a missionary and then abducted an Indian girl whom he then killed and devoured 'after cohabiting with her for some time' (130).

The journey concludes with the grim reflection that 'we ... would soon ... be treading the flinty city streets, and, divorced from Nature, become once more the bond-slaves of civilization' (146). A call to the reader follows: flee enervating luxury and hie to the spare and invigorating freedoms of the north. We are back to Canada First and to Robert G. Haliburton's *The men of the north*.[36]

The contradictions have not subsided, the dream remains unattainable. Even to discover the garden is to begin to destroy it. That is a tragedy greater than that of Tecumseh, than that of Loyalism even. Mair's work shows how difficult it was to face that loss, and how many the devices – personal and cultural – for trying to ignore it.

Interlude: *A Beautiful Rebel*

Sometimes a single work sums up many others; through it we can view the larger pattern. Wilfred Campbell's *A beautiful rebel: a romance of Canada in eighteen hundred and twelve* (1909) shows that the half-century between it and Kirby's *The U.E.* had neither altered the mythology of Loyalism nor lightened the stresses visited upon it by a changing society. This historical novel displays at once the covenantal sense of Kirby (including the garden with the nest of traitors) and the rootlessness found in the later work of Mair. In language and setting, the novel rests uneasily within an Upper Canadian space. It adopts the romantic mould cast by *The golden dog* for Canadian historical fiction; cracks appear in the finished product when we examine it. As in *Tecumseh*, awkward questions posed by the historical material are dismissed through romantic and rhetorical fantasy, though the dismissal does not make them disappear. *A beautiful rebel* at once sums up a process we have been observing and shows as well how a manner of viewing the history and destiny of Upper Canada has reached a point where its contradictions are wrecking it.

Written in the manner of Sir Walter Scott, the novel delineates the lives of its characters within a larger historical perspective. It follows Scott in employing individual fate as a symbolic device for the resolution of historic national conflicts and anomalies. Scott's novels displayed the romantic imagination's preoccupation with the outcast, with social groups left behind by history whose values, however obsolete, need to be recognized by their successors. The Englishmen in Canada who populate Campbell's novel are fossils of a bygone era, yet their heirs attempt to salvage the good in their heritage and use it towards survival within a new environment.

Briefly, the novel concerns the process by which Etherington, of clouded

English ancestry and a relative of the High Tory, would-be squire of Niagara, Colonel Monmouth, falls in love with the girl who gives the book its title. She is the offspring of Roundheads and Methodists. Though 1812 is his focus, Campbell draws out the larger dimensions of his conflict. We noted in Ryerson an appearance of the Cavalier versus Roundhead theory of the origins of the American Revolution. Campbell's authorial comment emphasizes this to the point of introducing an anachronistic reference to the u.s. Civil War into his discourse.† The 'disloyal harangue' of a Methodist preacher recalls revolutionary Boston (96), as do references to a Continental army and Tories on the part of Silas Fox, a late Loyalist villain-buffoon. The second act in the drama begun by the American Revolution is 1812, and loyalty comes to be equated with United Empire Loyalism (28). The frequent appearances of the terms loyal and disloyal in the text leave no doubt that the uELs hold a near-monopoly on the virtue. In sound, Family-Compact fashion Monmouth, who 'felt that, in a sense, he owned his tenants, for the majority of them had got their land from him,' is not himself a uEL (203). He is rather someone who uses the loyalty equals Loyalism formula to enshrine the repressive measures he takes in 1812. The war continues what 1775 began, though a new Upper Canadian theatre of war has been added.

Campbell, whose administrative responsibilities at the Canadian Archives in Ottawa included the uEL material, never quite settles into the reality it represented.‡ How else can we explain his description of an Anglican priest as a member of the established church (212)? However that may have gratified the dour shade of John Strachan, it did not apply to the Upper Canada of that time. This failure forms part of a larger problem, that of attempting to impose Old World canons of romantic behaviour upon the more prosaic milieu of the New. A perennial problem in the classic American literature of the nineteenth century (Poe and Hawthorne, for example), it becomes a jarring literary device in a writer of Campbell's abilities. The blond heroine, Diana Philpotts, suffers from a sensibility nurtured upon Gothick romances. Like Twain's Emmeline Grangerford, she views the North American scene through their eyes (167). In a similar fashion, Campbell gives his hard-scrabble frontier society its share of female faints and palpitations, along with operatic displays of high feeling (149, 188, 289, 108). Despite her Roundhead upbringing, the

† All references to the novel are from the edition by Westminster, Toronto 1909. The widespread appearance of the Cavalier vs Roundhead dichotomy in the mind of the American South, old and new, is treated in William R. Taylor, *Yankee and Cavalier: the Old South and American national character* (New York: George Braziller 1961).

‡ Carl F. Klink, *Wilfred Campbell, a study in provincial Victorianism* (Toronto: Ryerson 1942), 112–13.

beautiful rebel Lydia must be moulded into the shape of a romantic heroine. She therefore journeys in a shallop (169) in the manner of a Tennysonian maiden, recalling the faery barque appearing beneath the fantasized heights of Quebec City in Homer Watson's painting of *The Death of Elaine* (1877). She walks amid Arcadian imagery to a deep romantic chasm, but the jarring tone of the proceedings there (she hurls an enemy supply of muskets down the pit and then wakens a sleeping drunk by tossing a pot of water over him) shows how easily the grand gesture slides into the mean act (160–6). When Lydia's plight is compared to those of Mary Stuart and Lady Jane Grey, it is the image's remoteness from the actual experience which strikes the reader (228).

Why this high-falutin apparatus surrounding the daughter of a Niagara farmer? It creates a colonial Canada whose links with the motherland include the right to deck herself out in regal trappings. For this reason, the arrogant Monmouth – a name recalling both a rebel duke in history and the wealthy voluptuary in Disraeli's *Coningsby* – easily vanquishes the clownish Fox's threat to his manor. Monmouth suffers, after all, from a dark, Byronic flaw rendering him grandly heroic in his woe (310–11). Though we know nothing more of the secret than that it represents 'the terrible fate which overhangs so many of those of a certain strain of Old World heredity' we must surmise that it is a terrible fate indeed (312–13).† Campbell places the Bradfords' Methodist meeting in a garden and adorns Monmouth's estate with a similar pleasaunce to underline that his characters are not roughing it in the bush (88–9, 125). They have already made a garden of it. The young lovers, who never fully share in the arrogance of the Tories or the fanaticism of the Roundheads, become heirs to those gardens and the traditions of reconciliation and monarchist civility they imply. Theirs is the Upper Canada of frontier newness and opportunity plus the grace and elegance of imperial ties, this best of both worlds which we shall see later writers perceive with the pain of loss. '"We will here begin,"' Etherington tells Lydia, '"the great compromise, in which alone life in this young country can last."' Campbell drives the point home when he finds in 'their youth and their love, emblem of the young nation that was to be' (317). Their covenant between old and new will sustain the new society.

Campbell is aware of the complexities of fusing Old World with New. He introduces the well-to-do wastrel Tom Philpotts, son of a Royal Navy personage of considerable pretensions, leading him from treason to a prospective lifetime of drunkenness and marriage to a slut in order to indicate 'the irony of aristocratic fate, in its struggle with the idiosyncrasies of pioneer

† Have we here a euphemism for venereal disease?

conditions' (315). Yet Campbell's choice of romantic literary conventions and the attitudes he displays in his authorial commentary deter him from applying the lesson of Tom Philpotts to his own depiction of Upper Canadian realities.

Obviously, the conventions of the popular historical novel of the time compelled a certain grandiosity of approach, as the works of Sir Gilbert Parker attest. But the reader's discomfort does not arise from watching a captive dash through the woods with his hands bound behind him and then break his bonds by rubbing them against a tree trunk; that is a matter of artistic licence (255). What jars is the forcing of pioneer experience into an exaggeratedly heroic form that batters at our sense of the significance – homely, but no less worthy for that – of the historical experience.

The beliefs that hamper the author's handling of the experience can be seen in two passages. The first concerns Silas Fox after he has incurred the wrath of his followers:

But there is a always a minority which remains true to the fallen. This is the age of minorities, and they are, strange to say, regarded as sacred by those who most fondly worship the democracy which was founded on the rights of the majority. Majority rule was the fetish of the nineteenth century; now it is minority rule which is ideal. It is remarkable how soon mankind tires of its gods; so Mr. Fox found to his cost. But were it not for the faithful minorities, where would be the compensation for stricken greatness, shorn of its power, in this uncertain world, which so easily rejects its heroes? So in like manner as doth some modern political leader, rejected by his unappreciative country at the polls, who rolls out of the party scrimmage like an ill-used football, (victim of cruel fame and crueler fortune) did Captain Fox pick himself up both physically and morally, and discovered that, if fate had been unkind, he was not entirely forsaken. (201)

The mock-heroic simile at the conclusion holds greater interest than the political speculations preceding it. The language of the novel grows uneasy in tone whenever it reflects upon the idealized world of the past and the prosaic realities of its own time. Unable to employ modern idiom in a straightforward manner, yet equally powerless to come up with a better expression for what he wishes to say, the author daintily wraps a cliché within a disclaimer when he notes that a particular course of action, 'in a modern, vulgar, mercantile phrase, "fails to deliver the goods"' (199) . The lengthy passage cited above shows a similar rhetorical clumsiness. It assumes a frankly élitist view of political morality, a Loyalists-must-be-losers concept of a faithful remnant's devotion to the fallen. But it cannot follow through with the rhetorical implications of such a viewpoint and place Fox's discomfort within a serious framework. He is himself a joke, and his plight is aligned with that of another joke, the 'ill-used football' of a contemporary politician. Villainy reduced to buffoonery is an ancient rhetorical ploy, yet here the irony ultimately undermines the very attitudes the novel seeks to uphold – the supremacy of the faithful minority, loyal through thick and thin.

Three pages later in the novel, another passage entangles itself in its own ideas:

They were all good sturdy fellows, much like the best of Mr. Fox's 'regulators,' but with different convictions; and if indifferent soldiers, being more used to the plough and the axe, they were at least loyal, and had a strong prejudice against, and antipathy to what they called, 'those half-Yankee rebels.' If they had been asked what it all meant, they could not have answered, save that Colonel Monmouth knew, and that was enough for them. They were not great thinkers, not worrying over why one man was rich and another man poor, one great and another humble – as if such worrying had ever really produced any magic levelling; but they went to church or to 'meeting,' as it was called, cleared the forest, and did their duty to their families and themselves as sensible men should, as the parson put it weekly, 'in that state of life to which it had pleased God to call them.'

This shows that all sorts of people go to make up a world; that as there are two sides to a question, so there must be at least two parties in every community, not to speak of Churchmen and Chapel-goers, Roundheads and Cavaliers, Torys and Reformers, to the end of time. It would be a very uninteresting and dull world where there was no strife or argument, no hills to climb, no obstacles to overcome, with no consequent development of character and individuality. (204)

The opening paragraph stands as a consistent, if repellent, relegation of the majority of the people to a state of deferential cloddishness. However hoary the sentiment, it cannot be said to have deep root in Upper Canada, where only the most familially compacted of the gentry could ever have viewed the citizenry as content with blissful subordination. That kind of élitist thinking remains consistent with the novel's conventions, of course, whereby the tenors and sopranos sing more interesting passages than do the members of the chorus. But then the second paragraph brings forward a model of society based upon a liberal belief in the virtues of dialogue and dissent. The ethic of subordination and deference has been replaced with one that stresses conflict and disagreement. It is as jarring as if de Maistre began to cite *On liberty* as proof of his conclusions.

The inconsistencies within the two selected passages indicate the author's uncertainty about the socio-political environment he is addressing. The

Ontario Campbell lives in constitutes an unabashedly liberal, capitalist, and (abashedly) secularist society. If any literary convention uniquely suits the way this society perceives reality, then it is that of realism. The Upper Canada he depicts appears as an agrarian, deferential, and devout polity. Romance seems its characteristic mode of fictive discourse. Yet the one society grew out of the other. They are hardly discontinuous. The gap Campbell's prose style shows should not be there, unless something about the society's earlier state is being overlooked. The author and his creation are attempting to reside in two places that they have made out of what was in fact a single entity, and therefore a society's heritage becomes split from the facts of its present state.

A beautiful rebel reveals that the Loyalist paradigm of Upper Canadian experience can no longer attain a confident imaginative articulation. Though the novel deals with 1812 as a purely local affair and leaves the regular soldiers in the remote background, it still rests uneasily within its locality. Romantic conventions rather than historical fact govern the behaviour of its characters and the resolution of the story, while the author's commentary shows the split between what he sees as a poetic past and a prosaic present. The garden is saved, traitors expelled, the covenant affirmed, and a single vision of Anglo-Canada asserted. Social disturbance stems from enemies without and from traitors and the confused within. The last will always see reason once the true nature of their allies is revealed. The awkward question of whether a democratic or a hierarchical social vision is to prevail is ducked by a union of good hearts and young bodies. Yet the authorial commentary – intrusive, confused, anachronistic – testifies to the conflict between the social vision suggested by the narrative and the actualities of the realistic and pragmatic society that has come to be. A culture whose very nature downplays historical groundings in favour of change and material advancement is attempting to cast its origins into an idealized vision of timeless continuity. The result is strain and the adoption of a bogus past. The Loyalist image, the novel demonstrates, can no longer assert itself nakedly and explicitly as the model for a society's sense of selfhood. In the examination of the writings of Mazo de la Roche that follows, we will learn how the Loyalist vision appears in a more mediated and oblique fashion.

5 Mazo de la Roche: The Foundations of Jalna

The Loyalist myth forms the matrix of an Upper Canadian social vision, the foundation of a region's sense of selfhood. A host of variations and novelties can be piled atop it, but it stands as the eventual support of them all. We are not dealing with a cycle of myths, a narrative progress wherein one story of the gods flows inexorably from the preceding one. In pre-modern cultures, later mythographers and poets knit together the scattered stories into cyclic narratives. We, however, study a culture born in the modern era when a culture no longer directs its strongest imaginations toward that sort of grand synthesis. This loss of imaginative energy produces the many self-conscious, feeble attempts to figure forth 'The American epic.' Let *John Brown's Body* stand for the whole earnest crew. Students of American literaure find that the weightiest claims to be considered an American epic are those made by a work that is quirky, parodistic, pessimistic, and oblique, an old sea monster that staves in the ship of a national culture that values greatly the ordered and the optimistic.

This voyaging with *Moby-Dick* is not a distraction from our purported goal but serves as an introduction to a consideration of a matter not yet noted in Canadian criticism. We can observe how the output of a popular, formulaic, and sentimental author reflects in an unsystematic, displaced, yet detailed manner many elements of what we have been viewing as the Loyalist imagination. The Jalna chronicles of Mazo de la Roche (1879–1961) may come closer to soap opera than to literature, but they also tell us how firm remained the Loyalist model's grip over Ontario's sense of itself. While Canadian critics have rarely considered her work worthy of sustained attention, a body of fiction possessing sufficient world-wide popularity to have sold 11 million copies (9 million of them in hardcover) by 1966, merits some notice.[1] This cycle of an Ontario family within an Ontario setting sets forth in its fashion an Upper Canadian social vision whose contours resemble those of the Loyalist visions we have been examining. The social vision found in Jalna is neither coherent nor profound; its evasions and inadequacies are what reveal to us the nature of the culture Jalna defines. Recall how Richardson's *Wacousta* employs the conventions of Gothic and sentimental fiction to set forth a picture of terrorized social man, one whose pastoral yearnings are savaged by wilderness and garrison realities alike. 'Myself am Hell' could not only serve as the motto of the demonic yet tragic Wacousta, but of any representative Everyman in that novel. Ultimately, the space it seeks to embody becomes an interior one, and the bridge between forests and fort an uneasy meeting ground between two unhappy aspects of the human condition.

In the same way, one is forced finally to reduce Jalna to an imaginative status. It is at once a sustaining matrix for the Whiteoak family, and a magical spot that discloses the impossibility of their surviving anywhere else. 'Jalnaland,' as one critic terms it, calling attention to its resemblance to Disney's amusement parks, serves as an infinitely resilient cockpit for the fevered passions of its inmates.[2] Yet the more successfully it contains the anarchic forces within, the less credible it seems as an actual house. Therefore, Jalna comes to embody a style rather than define an actual physical space.

Did there actually exist after World War I, a group of people in the environs of Clarkson, Ontario, who lived like the English landed gentry? If we can believe the testimony both of Mazo and of her far more reliable young friend, Dorothy Livesay, there were at least those who sought to live in that fashion, and who considered that in fact they did.[3] Social history, however, is not my concern here, but rather the sort of fictional structure the author created to accommodate that sense of society, as well as the disembodied, ideal nature of the social vision implied. If, as her biographer points out, Mazo de la Roche served as 'chief mourner for the dying English influence in Canada,' then she also demonstrates how a Loyalist mythology (unable to place itself within a concrete modern context) can serve as a hidden foundation for a sentimentalized Upper Canada.[4]

I

The brief, perceptive note in Norah Story's *The Oxford companion to Canadian history and literature* indicates that Jalna's founding came about when the author imagined a matriarch, Adeline Whiteoak, large enough to fill that great, good place pre-Jalna fictions had erected. What do these early works tell us of the symbolic dimensions of Jalna itself? *Explorers of the Dawn* (1922), a collection of stories about a trio of brothers left in the care of a dragonish governess, is set in a sticky-sweet never-never land. There is more to this than formulaic psychology and diction, more than a cloying coziness. As Christopher Morley pointed out in his Foreword to the book, the author's hold on her setting is insecure.[5] Events take place in a spot that makes sense only as an Edwardian Barchester, yet the speech of the boys and certain other details belong to Canada. The lower orders are given to lubricious little malapropisms – ' "If I was to swape till I fell prostitute, I'd never git it clane" ' (236) – and the mischievous cuteness of magazine-fiction kiddies dribbles everywhere. Yet the vague, mid-Atlantic environment reveals a popular writer's imagination looking for a place to light.

By the time of *Possession* (1923), a spot closer to home had been found.[6] This time it is the fruit farm near Bronte, Ontario, in which the author spent some of her late adolescent years. Jalna begins to take shape as Derek, the new owner of the farm, finds it equipped with picturesque and happy retainers plus a clan of wandering Indians who serve as berry pickers at harvest time. Yet what could have turned out a rural idyll in the style of Kirby's *The U.E.* instead turns into a picture of the disastrous results of a liaison between the hero and an Indian child-woman. A vague sense of 'doing the right thing' and the pressure of local opinion force him into a rotten marriage. Financial failure looms at the story's end.

With its emphatic display of the dangers inherent in the pleasure principle, *Possession* could well serve as an archetypal piece of Canadian fiction. The ending remains equivocal: an implausible reunion of the couple follows the sudden death of their child, indicating that de la Roche did not fully intend for her story to leave the reader in the F.P. Groveish gloom it does. Despite throbbing, pseudo-Lawrentian passages on the passion linking earth and sky (64), the repressive gloom caused by a sense of the disasters inherent in sexuality itself pervades the novel.

Summing up her fiction as a whole, Desmond Pacey wrote that de la Roche's 'heroes ... are those who have managed to retain a fresh, instinctive, passionate response towards life.'[7] With *Delight* (1926), this passion becomes apparent. If the writer has discovered the successfully vivacious protagonist she will use throughout the Jalna series later on, she has not located the complementary setting she will later provide. The aptly named Delight Mainprize blooms as an object of universal desire within a squalid, small-town setting in the Niagara peninsula. So strong is the matriarchal fear and hatred of her sexuality that the townswomen nearly succeed in drowning her before she is saved by the man she is to marry. For all of its Perils-of-Pauline flights and escapes, the novel conveys a convincing and bitter picture of life in a rural slum. This and the later *Growth of a man* (1938) indicate the author's mastery of the dirt, boredom, and pettiness of such places. That realism links her back to Grove, and forward to our distinguished contemporary, Alice Munro.

The assault upon Delight's innocent but vibrant sexuality (for the novel's most erotic passage occurs when the heroine goes to bed with a treasured teapot†) reveals the author's Hardyesque sense of the penalties visited upon the lively and rebellious by their conventional and envious neighbours. The demands of realism would force any writer adopting its conventions to portray the wretchedness de la Roche did in *Delight*, but the happy ending she wrenched from the story despite its realism. Whether out of the adolescent quality of her imagination or her accommodation to the pop fiction market's requirement of happy endings, her next and most important fiction contained a setting in which her lively and rebellious protagonists could exercise their virtues without fear of reprisal. And one of the foundations of that enclosed world of secure non-conformity, of steamy passion alongside social conti-nuity, of Gothic thriller transformed into domestic idyll, proved to be an offshoot of the Loyalist myth.

II

As we have seen most clearly in the works of William Kirby, Loyalism is nothing if not covenantal in its moral assessment of politics. Fidelity produces counter-fidelity. Thus the colonial society flourishes amid the mother country's benevolence. Such a concept can acquire a mystical, even magical resonance, with little in the way of practical involvement. Though the Whiteoaks are not themselves Loyalists, they are unflaggingly loyal, commit-ted wholly to the advancement of British imperial aims. And for this, they expect consideration: 'Conditions like [the Great Depression] might be inevitable in Europe. If the United States were in a mess – well, they had only

---

† She could not bear to part with the [tea] pot tonight. She would lay it on the other pillow ... It would be company, a bedfellow, almost. She placed it snugly on the pillow, smiled at it tenderly, blew out the light, and got in beside it.

   It really was company in this lonely place. She laid one hand on its shiny fluted belly. Its spout curved toward her parted lips. (128)

themselves to blame. But Canada had done nothing to deserve this. She had been good; she had been loyal; she had spilled her blood when there was fighting to be done; and had minded her own business afterwards. Especially the family at Jalna did not deserve it. They had upheld the old traditions in the Province. They had stood by Jalna and stuck by each other. So they reasoned, and looked at one another baffled' (MOJ, chap. 8).[8] Our sense of the difference between author and creation blurs here, but no one can deny that the passage effectively conveys the mind-set, the barely articulated axiomata, of an apolitical, demanding, and inward-looking tribe. Economic and social realities disappear in a fog of moralizing. The maintenance of social codes ('the old traditions in the Province'), the preservation of family property ('They had stood by Jalna'), and family ties (they had 'stuck by each other') are deemed sufficient grounds for demanding shelter from a global cataclysm.

It has been this way from the beginning. In the letter a friend sends to Philip Whiteoak, founder of the clan, he is urged to settle in Upper Canada where an 'agreeable little settlement of *respectable* families is being formed. You and your talented lady ... would receive the welcome here that people of your consequence *merit*' (YR, 6). The final word may, in context, sound strange to our ears, but its usage remains appropriate. For the Whiteoaks, just to be themselves constitutes an achievement worthy of deference and respect. That is the burden of the entire series, except that the Old World assumption of social consequence equalling merit gives way to the moralism of the New. That moralism here acquires its legitimacy from a concept of loyalty that has become enough of a shibboleth in Upper Canada to be invoked whenever one's superior virtue gets proclaimed. To put it another way, there is something magical about this thing called loyalty. As a mark of honour, it covers whole nations who, like children, can be evaluated in terms of good and bad, by virtue of which they either mind their own business or become a bunch of nosy old Paul Prys. It adorns virtuous and noble families within the nations as well. What, if any, imaginative reality lies behind these invocations?

Before proceeding to answer that question, let us note that actual Loyalists appear in the Jalna series. In that collection of at times lurid, at times amiable, personal reminiscences and fantasies she called her autobiography, Mazo de la Roche took great care to mention her Loyalist ancestors.[9] Obviously, her possession of them was something important to her sense of self. Despite this, none of her principal characters has a UEL background. In describing a minor figure, a one-armed veteran of 1812, the author gives Elihu Busby an air of extremism: 'But his strongest prejudice was against the Americans. He was descended from United Empire Loyalists who had left affluence behind them in New England and escaped to Canada in the early days of the Revolution.

The persecutions they had suffered before they left rankled with amazing freshness in his mind, for he had drunk them in as a boy from his grandparents' relating' (BOJ, 14). Their loyalty to the queen is unshakeable, we are told, but their Loyalism consists largely of a set of negative and grandiose attitudes: 'They cherished an undying dislike of Americans and exaggerated the importance of the property they had left behind, two generations ago, in Pennsylvania' (MJ, 9). De la Roche is quite explicit in slotting the Busbys below the Whiteoaks on the social ladder. They dislike the Whiteoaks for their hoity-toity ways, and nothing more stamps the Busbys as non-gentry than their pro-Northern views about the American Civil War.[10]

De la Roche has taken the Loyalist myth and split it in order to produce a more genteel variation. Wilfred Campbell's *A beautiful rebel* began that process in fiction. It dealt with English gentry in Canada versus Americanized Canadians of Roundhead / Methodist leanings. Both Jalna and Monmouth's estate in *A beautiful rebel* possess a garden-like, paradisal air. Yet Campbell's novel remains far more explicit in its equation of loyalty with its specific embodiment in the political fact of United Empire Loyalism. Campbell's final union of his couple represents a reconciliation on Canadian soil of those aspects of our life that are inevitably North American with those that are undeniably British. That is hardly the aim of the Jalna series, which seeks to maintain the sequestered existence of Jalna as a near-British enclave in the province that her novels, as late as 1931, were still referring to as Upper Canada (FF, 4). When the recurrent Loyalist image of the garden of the Lord in Upper Canada first appeared, it sprang from a sense of the benefits and ties marking the specific historical processes of 1776, 1812, and 1837. Of course, we may describe the linking of these dates into a continuum as an example of a mythology. We may even employ that last word in a pejorative sense. But the dates, whatever we do with them, refer to actual historical events. The Jalna chronicles reveal, however, the ease with which the image of the covenantal life, the good life, and ultimately the genteel life can be split off from any historical grounding and yet maintain itself as a powerful imaginative force. To be sure, images of the good life need not be grounded in specific historical events, unless one believes in the literal truth of the second chapter of Genesis. Yet in de la Roche we have the heritage-conscious product of a culture where the Loyalist myth had played a major role in the shaping of its image of well-being. In her work we can observe a process through which a specific historical experience feeds into the broader stream of visions about the nature of the good life.

The defence of the lifestyle (as we would term it) that the Jalna property embodies burns at the imaginative core of the series. Again and again, individual Whiteoaks justify their existence, personal and collective, not in terms of historical and political realities, but in terms of how closely they have kept the faith: Jalna was acquired 'in order that those who valued privacy and their heritage of British tradition, might enjoy both here' (RTJ, 14); the ancestors 'wanted to lead contented peaceful lives and teach their children to fear God, honour the Queen, fight for her if necessary. In short, behave like gentlemen' (MW, 5).[11] When I told him I was engaged in a study of Upper Canadian Loyalism, a friend of mine remarked, 'Well, it's two things: the actual Loyalists, and the squirarchy.' Of course, it is this later appropriation of Loyalism for the purpose of defending an idealized social system that we are concerned with here.[12]

But the reader must not move too quickly in identifying this imaginative tactic with the ploys of John Strachan and John Beverley Robinson in their equation of deference to the rulers of the Family Compact with the historical fact of Loyalism. There exists, to be sure, a certain likeness between their brazen appropriation and de la Roche's imaginative sleight-of-hand. Behind her cultural enterprise, however, stands an attempt to grant a spiritual dimension and justification for a set of social facts, as is the case with the sense of Upper Canada in Mrs Moodie's accounts of life in the bush. Her struggle to maintain civilized living standards amid besotted settlers, many of them of Loyalist origin, dovetails with Tiger Dunlop's besotted attempt at a squirarchy at Goderich.[13]

Yet Jalna as an imaginative creation comes long after such dreams reflected a powerful social force in the province. Jalna remains a nostalgic extrapolation from a few Ontario houses of a would-be dominant lifestyle. What it stood for had quite fallen by the wayside in a Canada dominated by an aggressive, entrepreneurial system waxing fat from banks and insurance companies, railways, mercantile houses, and the exploitation of non-renewable resources. The canons of popular serial fiction shaped the contours of the dream that is Jalna, which places it even farther away from reality than the self-serving paradigms of a ruling élite. Those devices of popular story-telling, however, will swing round these tales of the manor to a direction familiar to us from the more explicitly Loyalist works we have examined. To study the narrative structure of the Jalna series in fact bridges the familiar Loyalism versus loyalty split.

III

Why make false apologies about the narrative aspects of the Jalna series? The stories resemble nothing so much as soap opera: they concern themselves with a single family and the folk who swing into its orbit. Nothing occupies any member of the family so much as another member's actions and motivations. Everyone has ample leisure to dissect family affairs, many of them of an erotic or financial nature. Talks about sex and money are sure-fire devices for holding a reader's attention. The rituals of family life – especially those of mealtime, for which the Whiteoaks hold a particular affection – get loving and frequent observation, and the ending of each novel remains sufficiently open to demand a credible and fascinating successor. The simplicity of the characters themselves and the audience's lengthy acquaintance with them assures that their responses to situations become quite predictable. Thus the specific nature of the current crisis provides the novel element in each new installment.

The author's handicap became her strength here. She had begun the series under the drawback of including specific dates and ages.[14] This forced her to fill in gaps as well as to move ahead in a regular sequential pattern. Normal chronology existed for only the first four novels, and she then began filling in the past. This in turn made for a more varied and entertaining series, since for the second half she alternated her production between present-day stories and past ones. Her strength as a popular writer lay in more than her ability to create vivid characters and place them in situations often of a perverse and titillating sort. She was also able to exert great imaginative force in the construction of a dwelling and to make that house and the people in it embody an idealized social vision. It is this generally unacknowledged skill of hers that lifts the series into whatever height it maintains above ordinary soap operas. As her first editor at Atlantic, Little, Brown pointed out, Jalna itself was the hero of the initial novel.[15] Her ability to sustain that fact and all it entails through another fifteen novels testifies to the special nature of her serial fiction.

What then happens in a typical Jalna romance? Discovering this will reveal those technical aspects of the series that reinforce the social aspects that most concern me. In a typical volume, some threat is posed to Jalna and the Whiteoaks either by an outside force (a stock fraud, a developer, the Depression, World War II) or by some family conflict (fraternal rivalries, especially in sexual matters, marital discord, headstrong children). Various members of the family flag in their devotion to the place, though Gran (Adeline), the matriarch, and her grandson Renny, who follows her as master of Jalna, never waver. Following a series of meals, family gatherings, cabals, emotional crises, and usually a trip elsewhere by some member or other, a near-miraculous factor, often of a monetary sort, will alleviate the threat and restore harmony. Yes, Jalna is a garrison, appropriately enough since it is named after its officer founder's last Indian station.

We have seen how Jalna's inhabitants assume the role of defenders of a social tradition. What also strikes the reader is a kind of Richardsonian psychic affinity that also distinguishes the family. The property – which as one character points out, is a Canadian estate and not a dukedom (CJ 15) – bears the distinctly Richardsonian feature of a bridge between its two parts, where lovers are forever assembling for trysts and the troubled repair to when in need of solitude or meditation. Psychological bridges are of greater significance, since the Whiteoaks' strongest feelings are expressed to their kin rather than to spouses or friends. No reader can ignore the toying with homosexuality and incest in the novels. While this certainly owes something to a popular writer's gift for titillation, it also denotes a characteristic attitude of de la Roche that cannot be attributed to calculation alone. Throughout her fiction, two people going to bed together are generally of the same sex. In the Jalna books, it becomes the mark of strong family feeling (with doubtless a host of erotic ramifications that remain displaced and unexplored), the sense of kinship making the Whiteoaks a race apart (see YR, 29). Since, we are told, 'no outside contacts modified the pungent vitality of their relations with each other' (J, 15), it comes as but a slight surprise that Renny quits his wife's bed to sleep with his lonely younger brother, reassuring the fearful lad that a dozen wives could not come between them (FF, 2, 19).† No wonder that the author initially provided too few bedrooms to provide for strictly moral sleeping arrangements for her characters, an embarrassment from which she was saved by an alert editorial assistant.[16]

The first novel, the most carefully structured of all, is a domesticated Gothic thriller, in which the sheltered outsider from New York arrives as a bride in the house of her husband's eccentric relatives. The matriarch, Gran, enjoys nothing so much as eating and watching boys being flogged (J, 2, 20). In the same manner that Richardson adopted, this closed world of family-bound feelings overflows with instances of voyeurism. No one in the Jalna series falls in love and forthrightly declares it. They must first be spied on by someone stumbling upon their rendezvous, perhaps even someone who has first staked out the place to catch them. While the novels follow the then-filmland custom of having sexual union take place between the kiss that closes the chapter and the Roman numeral announcing the next, its preliminaries or aftermath frequently include being secretly observed.

Enough has been said to indicate the affinities of the world of Major Richardson with Jalna. Of course, any full perspective would have to include the tragic dimensions of Richardson's Gothic, where the terror-filled

---

† Earlier in the series, we find the two young men busy at a game of Bride and Groom (J, 13).

wilderness and the narcissistic garrison exhaust between them the possibilities for human fulfilment. Jalna remains soap opera rather than melodrama. Thus, a host of potentially disturbing phenomena are touched on, only to be integrated into the endless tale of familiar events in the familiar mansion that removes their sting. Soap opera requires that an audience remain in tune with the complicated family quarrels and stresses by the frequent recapitulation of events. At the same time, this narrative device gains the added effect of strengthening the readers' sense of the inward-looking, self-sufficient nature of the Whiteoak world. Since a way of viewing society and the imaginative reality of Upper Canada forms a theme of the series, the series' structure emphasizes its similarity to the achievement of Major Richardson. How ironic that the myth of assured, Anglo-Canadian gentry should in its form recall the vision of beleaguered Loyalist Canada caught in Richardson's pages.

IV

Within that enclosed space of Jalna, little happens that does not eventually reaffirm the goodness of the place. The Whiteoaks are forever journeying to New York, Britain, and Ireland, only to return with whatever friends or lovers they have collected. Their fidelity guarantees them a seat among the elect, and religion for them is a social piety, more self-worship than ancestor-worship. Old Philip Whiteoak, founder of the clan, donated the land on which stands the church he built; Renny's weekly reading of the Lessons seems as necessary and fitting a portion of the service as the General Confession. It is all cheerfully Erastian, in the finest traditions of the Church of England. Of course the church of Jalna does not uphold the state directly, but the Whiteoak claim to the special care of Providence on account of their allegiance to the remote imperial power. We are told that the Whiteoaks remain 'such confirmed royalists' that a hymn's praise of 'My God and King' might well have seemed to them a proclamation of 'their allegiance to George V' (WB, 22). They keep religion in its place, never saying a grace before the meals they are forever consuming. As Renny's wife, Alayne, notes, their 'hidebound traditions' are those 'of family, of church-going, of male superiority' (HARVEST, 4), and it is in terms of this concern that their religious exercises are conducted. They are covenantal rituals, garrison church parades, devoid of any doctrinal content.

The idol appeased by these exercises remains Gran Whiteoak. With her obstinacy, greed, and pride, her ceaseless round of consumption and ingestion, she recalls the great white mother of Victorian England, a figure at once parasitic and prolific to whom affection and sentiment flow without great visible return. So much emphasis is placed upon her Indian shawls and the running gag of her Hindi-shrieking parrot that the hint of Gran as empress of India reinforces our sense of her as Victoria R. Her passing, midway through the second novel, made it all the more important for her creator to reverse chronology from time to time to bring back this most popular of her characters. Her looming background presence, the fact that the name of Adeline gets carried on in Renny's high-spirited daughter who comes to sleep in her grandmother's bed, all this structures family power according to the demands of fantasy. Renny, the ultra-masculine patriarch who generally smells of his stables, can always invoke the still-living presence of the vivid old matriarch, thus bestowing an all-inclusive sexuality on the ruling force of Jalna.

Inclusiveness and continuity mark life at Jalna. This doubtless accounts for the series' exceptional popularity in the Europe of the 1940s, as the author's fan mail testifies. Inclusiveness explains the ease with which Jalna itself or other dwellings on the estate manage to take in anyone whose presence the brothers desire. Continuity is affirmed not only by the house itself, but by the longevity the author grants her creations. Their unflagging interest in each other's business and the way in which the trials of the younger generation often parallel those of the older reinforce the sense of a seamless web of experience. Serial fiction and drama convey this sense of continuity as one of their chief delights; the Jalna formula reflects not merely a cynical calculation of just how much sameness the author can get away with, it is also an assessment of what expectations the audience brings to the event.

The idealized image of Upper Canada evoked by the Jalna series emphasizes stability, self-containment and continuity. Though this is dictated by the demands of serial fiction, it also appears to be the author's intention, in that endurance forms a principal theme of the book. The social implications of the narrative come from more than a politics dictated by literary form. For example, Loyalism itself stresses inclusiveness and reshapes history to that end: the Loyalist wars are stretched to include 1837, those of English birth who fought in 1812 appear as Loyalists, and the crest of the UEL Association crosses red hand with white to indicate its bi-racial nature. A sense of inclusiveness also marks Jalna. The mystical union between patriarchal and matriarchal figures has already been noted and is graphically conveyed by the fact that after Gran's death, Renny often sleeps in her bed. Beyond this image of inclusiveness, as well as the various generations of

Whiteoaks who nestle together in their oyster bed of a house, exists the emotional inclusiveness of the family. The series provides those dramatic highs and lows that the popular fictional form demands, but it also stresses the continuity of family life. Tantrums, infidelities, confrontations, revelations of hidden parentage, histrionic comings and goings: none of these halt family life and ritual. [17]

Another aspect of Whiteoak inclusiveness shows itself in the personalities of the brothers: Renny, the patriarchal womanizer and horse-tamer; Piers, the quick-tempered, grasping farmer; Wakefield, the intense, one-time monk who transforms himself into a successful actor at the drop of a cassock; Eden, the *poète maudit* who dies of tuberculosis; and Finch, the tortured artist, composer, and performer of music vaguely described but surely MGM-Rachmaninoff. Finch, with whom the author closely identified, stands as a clichéd re-creation of a romantic archetype. [18] Moody, naive, improvident (*Finch's fortune* concerns the way he allows much of his inheritance from Gran to slip away), unfeeling toward his son (CJ, 20–1), he plays moodily his role of Chopin among the Jorrockses. Eden is Finch's Hyde, a trifler in love and a ruthless if lovable sponger until his early death. The message is a simple one: the Whiteoaks as a family can survive anything. Their collective self-absorption lets them accommodate a wide range of what they must see as aberrant feelings and behaviour, mostly because they hold their collective worth in such high regard. Alayne, with her Emerson-and-water upbringing cannot faze them: 'her New England love of order, of seemliness, cried out against the disorder, the muddle-headedness of the Whiteoaks,' failing to see that '"we all love England; that is what matters"' (WOJ, 13, 26).

The reiterated claims to uniqueness turn potential threats into matters of mere narrative variety and titillation. So long as the covenant is kept, the social organism abides. The Virginia creeper covering Jalna itself speaks to this: clinging, ever burgeoning, threatening at times to cover the house entirely, it none the less each fall bursts into flaming colours that make the house seem glorious (VWJ, 8). [19]

To return to Desmond Pacey's comment, Jalna gave Mazo de la Roche an imaginary kingdom in which the threats posed to social peace by appetite and individualism could be safely absorbed and contained. So long as the house stands, the pleasure principle and the Whiteoaks' fascinating follies in the pursuit of it never become wholly destructive. An adolescent wish-fulfilment fantasy, it is called a paradise (BOJ, 8), one in which the snake of vitality and change can be accommodated without fatal disruption. Of course, that sort of bliss has its price.

V

Maintaining the self-sufficiency and inclusiveness of Jalna requires a system of priorities, no more clearly shown than in a description of a fountain on the property donated by one of the aged uncles. The decorative motifs include the figure of a Hindu (recalling the Indian posting of the founders), an Irish harp (Gran's Anglo-Irish Ascendancy background), and a British lion. ' "Canada," ' Uncle Nick announces dryly, ' "supplies the water" ' (HERITAGE, 9). Canada supplies the land and the living for the family, but Renny, despite his attendance at Royal Military College in Kingston, Ontario, fights both world wars in a British regiment whose depot is in England (WC, 21). Of course, the term ' "nationalism" had not occurred to him. He saw no stigma in the word "colonialism" ' (CJ, 29). The Canada of Eden's poetry consists of Group-of-Seven northern solitudes and the romantic history of New France, including a Kirbyesque meditation on 'The loves of Bigot' (J, 9; FF, 9). As her history of the port of Quebec reveals, this is also the Canada of the author: romantic French heroes, Loyalism and the War of 1812, and asides as to the real-life figures on whom she based her fictional characters.[20]

The USA would appear to be divided between the New England finickiness of Alayne and the mob-pollution of New York (WOJ, 11, 13). Crooked stockbrokers are New York based, though Finch's surest way to impress his brothers is to mention the size of his critical reputation in the States (WB, passim; RD, 11). The officer class founding Jalna and the adjoining Vaughan-lands wanted Upper Canada restricted to those of British stock. Runaway blacks are allowed to maintain their own settlements, where they may follow their overdone and unseemly religious practices (MJ, 19–21). Mixed bloods are cunning and dangerous; racial purity is a necessity if the country is to see 'freedom and integrity in the land' (BJ, 10, 8). Renny finds himself upset at the thought of his adolescent daughter not only seeing *Othello*, but watching a Negro actor (Paul Robeson) in the title role (RTJ, 20). The preservation of Jalna entails a constant warfare with neighbours seeking to erect subdivisions on its border (RD concerns itself especially with this, but variations on it run throughout the series), as well as with highway departments threatening to cut down trees. Many things, then, must of necessity be excluded if the freedom and spaciousness of Jalna are to be maintained.

Yet not even Miss Havisham could keep out time. The trees do not disappear, and a providential death insures the defeat of the scheme to erect Clappertown near Jalna, yet modernity intrudes finally in the form of pop music over the radio: 'the first brutal blare of a band playing an American version of native African music.' Finally even a television aerial flaunts itself above the roof-tops, tempting the children to watch wrestling rather than listen to Mozart (vwj, 5, 19). Because the other side has won, the cultural forces that once resisted modernity have been labelled with the highly emotive epithets of the victors. 'Backward-looking,' 'reactionary': these are the labels such forces must live with now. My aim is not to brand the sensibility of de la Roche with those terms but to note that her formula for keeping significant change at bay within a dream Upper Canada, that is Jalna itself, cannot resist the incursions of a culture that destroyed even the possibility of that dream. Was it that sense of defeat and the retreat to a dream world that made her autobiography so blank about the many years in Canada between her return from England and its publication? There ought to be a neutral word that denotes a state of looking backward without nostalgia, since looking forward is no longer considered the equivalent to gazing upon a prospect of advancing progress. The fact is this: despite the dreamy, debased, formulaic, and at times silly nature of Jalnaland, it stands as the ultimate in the popularization of a cast of mind important in the culture and history of Upper Canada. In the self-deprecating way of the colonial, Renny expresses his pride in his house's centenary by noting: ' "It's seldom that the same family lives in the same house for a century. Of course that's not long in the Old Country ... " ' Earlier in the book, the author has the house itself declare that ' " I will remain here, to justify your lives, *as long as this country survives*" ' (cj, 32, 1). I have added my own emphasis to the final words, because by 1958 even a Jalna romance had to take such hesitations into account. The sort of country that would support a Jalna, the sort of justification its survival gives to the way of life of those living there cannot be guaranteed even in the dream world of popular romance. Inclusiveness within, exclusivity without, yet the acreage still shrinks. Time does not stop.

VI

From 23 January to 30 April 1972, cbc-tv ran its ill-fated version of 'Jalna.' An expensive and elaborate series, planned as Canada's entry in the great television serialization stakes that followed upon the success of such bbc blockbusters as 'The Forsyte saga' and 'Upstairs, downstairs,' the production failed dismally. Extensive planning and negotiating over rights (with con- siderable diplomacy and circumspection, as *The secret of Jalna* reveals), the assembly of an all-star cast, the use of elaborate sets and locations: these could not save it.[21] Many reasons might be adduced for the failure, yet certainly one of them remains the production's arty and modernist treatment of chronology. Unannounced flashbacks and a general effort to 'layer' time rather than present the work in chronological sequence not only bewildered the viewer, but imposed upon the material a more sophisticated, modernist approach than suited it. However greatly that sort of approach may have appealed to the sensibilities of contemporary media persons, it deprived the audience of those comforts of continuity and painless simplicity which brought them to the Jalna books in the first place.

The vision of the great, good place that is the Jalna series attempts to assert the permanence of the threatened paradise and the abiding nature of a scarcely articulated social compact. '"This wilderness?"' scornfully asks a romantic wanderer through Jalna. It is '"already [in 1858] a close conventional community"' (BOJ, 9). And so it is, exactly as the Whiteoaks and their creator wanted it to be. It is the garden in the wilderness. It revels in its cultural strength, its ability to contain anarchic and destructive forces and turn them toward the enhancement of the family and their place. Jalna stands, finally, as a place of reconciliation.

Recall Charles Mair's *Tecumseh* and its distant backdrop of an uncivilized west whose solitudes can satisfy the yearnings civilization cannot; then summon up Kirby's New France, with its irreconcilable conflict between colonial simplicity and metropolitan greed. Remember also the tragic clash on Richardson's bridge between garrison and wilderness. At that point we can understand the function of Jalna and the means by which it put forward a sentimental solution to the Loyalist dilemma. The reconciliation is neither rightly nor convincingly earned. It depends upon an immature and melodramatic fudging of potentially disruptive conflicts by means of providential deaths, inheritance, and the timely release of crucial information. But we can see what the reconciliation is all about: the attempt to assert a civilized and imaginative account of (Upper) Canadian history.

Based upon the writers treated thus far, would it not be possible to view Loyalism (with its 'squirarchy' offshoot) as *the* social mythology of Upper Canada? To be sure, many other traditions reinforced that myth, but the bedrock historical process lay in the redemption of a new land by committed exiles. The image of the garden was always with us, a perpetually threatened garden in need of defenders. It is this vision which makes the impossibility of the garden so painful to the Richardsonian imagination. The pattern of suffering, redemption, and fulfilment through a compact (perpetually renewed through struggle and the preservation of traditions of culture and social custom) gives the myth a resonance humming throughout our literature from epic and closet drama to serial and historical fiction. The profoundly civilized nature of the myth makes it especially visible at a time when our artists seek the bush, the native peoples, and the animal as their imaginative markers. Yet a sense of loss for the destruction of the culture that produced that myth will continue in our literature. In fact, the pain of the loss of the garden to the wilderness will form the subject of subsequent chapters.

6 *The Reification of Loyalism*

During the years when the fiction of Mazo de la Roche appeared, Ontario was reifying its Loyalist heritage: the literary enterprise ceased to treat the past of Upper Canada in the language the culture once employed habitually. Instead of the rhetoric of moralism, that of pragmatism came to hold sway. This was not a cultural victory. Rather than a process of demythologizing and demystification, this occurrence simply substituted one kind of rhetoric for another as the Loyalist myth was subsumed within one of pioneering. Since the pioneer myth can be couched in terms of the practical and technical, it seems at first a more realistic model of experience. And it is – though not in the metaphysical and normative sense the term is usually employed to express. Just as 'realistic' also denotes an artistic convention which handles events in what remains ultimately no more 'real' a fashion than does symbolism, so it is with the 'realization' of the Loyalist heritage. That reification belongs itself to a process by which a culture comes to view its history within a new model of description, rather than through any discarding of an ancestral model of historical progression.

The works studied reveal that the ancestors are still with us, and in that sense they continue to assert a vision of continuity and relevance that formed the foundation of earlier texts. Yet the loss of a moralistic vocabulary cannot be left unnoticed because it means that it is no longer possible to put forward the Loyalist experience as a cultural ideal. It becomes instead another example of the way in which our culture once viewed itself, one of the many competitors in the struggle for mythical hegemony.

Jalna demonstrated the extent to which Loyalism had grown almost unnoticed, serving as a buried cornerstone for a social vision that had become sufficiently idealized to function in a sentimental and nostalgic fashion. The works that follow tell of another way in which that experience ceased to function with any considerable moral authority of its own, and became instead a regional variant within a continental myth of pioneering and the frontier.

I

The form of the Loyalist myth suggests a Christian *typos* of suffering (the Revolution), redemption (the acquisition of Canada), and ultimate vindication (success in 1812, material growth), all in the service of a covenant (fealty to crown and British institutions brings national survival under imperial aegis). The description of the Loyalist experience in religious and scriptural terminology owes its origins to Christianity and romanticism alike. The presence of the former needs little explanation. The America of the Puritans was the New Canaan, the refuge for the elect who had fled Egypt. More than a habit of speech, it served as the embodiment of the sacral mode of viewing American experience. It formed a salient feature of a national mode of discourse which came to have far-reaching consequences in American culture.[1] Loyalists simply proved themselves good, inescapably good, Americans in extending the tradition to include their particular variant. In acknowledging the Christian roots of the Loyalist myth, we do well to realize that it bears also the marks of the cultural revolution that shook the west at the end of the eighteenth century. For the pattern remains a displacement of a scriptural pattern of defining experience into a secular terminology locating the good in mundane rather than other-worldly terms. As the writings of Fellows and Barkley make clear, the structure of the Loyalist myth outlines a process of defeat, exile, hardship, and struggle which is followed by eventual and righteous triumph.[2] Prometheus unbound. Whatever this secularization of sacred history owes to the romantic revolt, the image of the outcast-now-victor so close to the heart of romantic culture gave the myth a special appeal, and perhaps a deceptive one. While the culture of Upper Canada remained materialistic, absorbed in the exploitation of the environment and the realization of prosperity, its collective sense of what had made it great expressed itself in an other-worldly vocabulary. To stroll along Jarvis Street in Toronto today is to recognize the solidity and pervasiveness of that mode of discourse in the Gothic mini-cathedrals that celebrate the union of the new acquisitiveness and the historic pieties.[3] Of course, that cultural synthesis was not to last, as the rolls of those churches' congregations attest.

To follow that synthesis from beginning to breakdown where Loyalism is concerned, let us begin with a collection of poems written during the Revolutionary period. There the language of religious experience describes the evil of the enemy and the injustice of the Loyalists' plight. They are counterblasts to the rebel literary assault. With its great debt to the English radical and commonwealth tradition, the language of the American Revolution was a scriptural one. When the Tory opposition consigns its enemies to perdition, it marks another skirmish in the holy war that is being waged. These poetic visions of rebel conventicles plotting their literally hellish schemes reminds us of the extent to which American Loyalists followed the low Miltonic road trodden by the Tory satirists of Britain, by Dryden, Swift, Pope, and the Scriblerus Group. Briefly, in these satirists the awesome (in Milton) evocations of the forces of evil have descended to the ironic juxtaposition of the mean in the sublime setting. For example, though the bathetic figures of Pope's *Dunciad* pursue their tasks of cultural demolition, the reader takes seriously only the attitudes they represent; their activities he can only view as comically obscene.

This sort of presentation demands a complex response of the reader, who cannot allow his amusement at the triflers to dilute his chagrin at the wreckage they bring about. Presumably, the American Tory poets sought to impart a similar experience; their use of religious setting and imagery strives to arouse in their audience something of the horror they would feel in the presence of actual blasphemy and impiety. The devices – and this is the difficulty – possess no more than an æsthetic value. A century of cultural change from the time of Milton has made angelic conclaves impossible for sophisticated audiences to accept literally. We are reading an ideological poetry whose very vocabulary occupies an uneasy middle ground between the actual and the symbolic. The means for expressing detestation and horror consist of a set of images, few of which can be taken wholly seriously in themselves.[4]

Yet the religious imagery can convince, as for example when it melds sacred and secular:

> Now, all compos'd, from danger far,
> I hear no more the din of war;
> > Nor shudder at alarms:
> But safely sink each night to rest, –
> No malice rankling through my breast, –
> > In Freedom's fostering arms.
>
> Tho' stripped of most the world admires,
> Yet torn by few untam'd desires,

> I rest in calm content;
> And humbly hope a gracious Lord
> Again those blessings will afford,
>   Which once his bounty lent.[5]

Sacred and secular pieties coalesce in a way that resembles those veiled, classical maidens embracing Christian crosses in nineteenth-century funerary art. One almost discerns the grandly Juno-esque person of Freedom enfolding the poet, who none the less continues to beseech the Lord for a restoration of the blessings he abandoned with such equanimity. Stoic impassivity and evangelical familiarity with a gentle Deity have met and mated.

The pace of material growth would shift the literature of Upper Canada into the recognition of it as a mark of divine favour. This sense of providence manifesting itself through progress animates a letter by Michael Grass to the *Kingston Gazette* in 1811. After praising 'HE who causeth the wilderness to smile and blossom like a rose,' it continues:

Seven and twenty years ago, scarce the vestige of a human habitation could be found in the whole extent of the Bay of Quinta! – Not a settler had dared to penetrate the vast forests that skirted its shores – Even on this spot, now governed with stately edifices, were to be seen only the bark-thatched wigwam of the savage, or the newly erected tent of the hardy loyalist – 'Then when the ear heard me it blessed me,' for strong in my attachment to my sovereign, and high in the confidence of my fellow subjects, I led the loyal band, I pointed out to them the scite of their future metropolis, and gained for persecuted principles a sanctuary[,] for myself and followers a home.[6]

Grass had been a captain of a New York militia company and a leader of the first Loyalist arrivals at the Bay of Quinte. His statements show the ability with which an educated person of his time conflated sacred with secular habits of expression. He not only reserves for himself the role of Moses, but completes the letter quoted from (it began as an *ubi sunt* lament) by making a complaint about the state of the public roads.[7] Only a robust sensibility can with such ease range through that width of human experience; it indicates the extent to which sacred and secular modes of discourse had merged to form a commonplace rhetoric for assessing Loyalism's triumphs. In the hands of the less skilled, this could be pushed to the extreme of an 1859 obituary. Here appears the conviction of the bishop of New Brunswick that pioneer longevity constituted 'a striking instance of the fulfillment of the promise contained in the fifth commandment, embracing as the commandment unquestionably does, the duty of obedience to civil rulers.'[8] A nineteenth-century historian, George Hodgins, would attribute to the Loyalists what looks now like a great chain-of-being concept of political allegiance.[9] Why therefore should not a contemporary of his, during a threnody on 1812, ring the changes on Scripture?

The first settlers on the soil were the American loyalists, men of educated and elevated minds, who had undergone trials and persecutions ... who exclaimed in the affecting language of the Psalmist 'When I forget thee, O Jerusalem, may my right hand forget its cunning.' They had left home, and friends, and wealth, and station, for a principle sanctified by its disinterestedness, and by the cunning of their hands enshrined it in the heart of the wilderness. They had borne, for long, the scoffs and jeers of neighbours ... The reflections of the past had been to these men the only – the proud reward of rare sufferings and sacrifices.

The writer, William Coffin, then equates the UELS' ceaseless carping on their suffering with 'the rapture with which the martyrs ... glory in the scenes of their martyrdom.' For this reason, 'the loud hosanna is often on their lips.'[10]

The overt scriptural echoes would resound as late as 1898, with Colonel George T. Denison of Canada First quoting Kirby's 1884 address describing the Loyalist migration in terms recalling both the scriptural and Virgilian exodus. Yet the Methodist bishop and popular historian William Withrow could show that by 1876 the triumph need no longer be couched in religious terms: 'The wilderness soon began to give place to smiling farms, thriving settlements, and waving fields of grain ... '[11] The foreshadowing in the final clause of the u.s. patriotic hymn, *America the Beautiful* (1895, 'for amber waves of grain') reminds us that the national polity came to replace the heavenly city as an object of ideal devotion. And the wilderness need no longer be invoked in an allegorical fashion. That is, the attentive reader will catch the ancient image, but it is not explicitly invoked. In 1877, another popular historian urges his readers to 'look with reverence upon this little band of prophets,' but then makes no more than a vague reference to 'great things' that have issued from such 'small beginnings.'[12] Perhaps that very passage reveals a microcosm of the process I am studying, in which we watch a shift from traditional pieties to the new, vaguer ones of an idealistic nationalism.

Along with that idealist sense of national destiny and aspiration would come an ever-widening gap between those hopes and the rough necessities engendered by pride and appetite. That is why in 1897 two history textbooks could employ very different vocabularies in summing up the Loyalist

achievement. W.H.P. Clement's *History of the dominion of Canada* concludes with a note of modest secular triumph, the sort one can imagine
being sounded by the burghers of Sara Jeannette Duncan's Elgin: '[The
settlers] fought their way through much discouragement to comfort and even
affluence.' Another textbook summation, however, reminds us of nothing so
much as the rhetoric of Lorne Murchison in Duncan's novel. Sir Charles
G.D. Roberts' *A history of Canada* asserts that 'as we watch the destiny of
this people taking shape, we shall be forced to realize that the hands most
potent in shaping it are the hands of the sons of the loyalists.'[13] The one-time
people of the Lord have become their own masters, hewers no longer of wood
but of their own destiny. An incantatory phrase like 'the destiny of this
people' stands for the sort of thinking that will dominate political life for the
next three-quarters of a century. The concept, thoroughly abstract and
thoroughly secular, does not convey even the hazy notion of meals, warmth,
and money in the bank found in Clement's 'comfort and even affluence.'

The wheel has swung full circle, with a new, quasi-religious rhetoric
substituted for the scriptural. Alongside this, however, stands an exclusively
materialist vocabulary by which national worth can be measured.[14] Can the
Loyalist achievement be made to fit into both languages?

II

If the split in language reflects a gap as wide as that between grace and nature, a
similar duality occurs in popular historical fiction about the Loyalist
experience. Here it falls along the lines of romantic versus realistic modes of
plot and characterization.[15] The consideration of *A beautiful rebel* revealed
this and serves as a fitting background for a survey of the way in which
Campbell's romance gave way to realism in the treatment of Loyalism.

Much of the fiction is concerned with violence and remains monitory in
tone. On the one hand, it follows the Upper Canadian military myth of
Loyalism, largely ignoring the non-violent pastoral of the Maritimes. Some
boys' books, for example, even though set in the Maritimes, feature
Loyalism's violent aspects, but then a reader expects that of such fiction.[16]
The war of 1812 and its attendant violence forms a continuous pattern in the
fiction. The monitory tone stems from a widespread conviction that a heritage
is being forgotten, a process which the novel seeks to reverse. In her preface to
The shadow of tradition: a tale of old Glengarry (1927), Carrie Holmes
MacGillivray speaks for a number of writers in declaring: 'In the short space

of a hundred and forty years the whole face of the country has been changed, and the trials and struggles of the pioneers are largely forgotten.'[17]

The threats posed by the passage of time, social change, and the Americanization of Canadian culture (the last so abiding a feature of the Canadian experience) would naturally lie behind much popular fiction.[18] To express those fears gives a moral seriousness to the imaginative project. Since Loyalism is perceived as the answer to one sort of threat in the past, the use of it as a subject implicitly asserts its relevance to those of the present. Thus in many ways *A beautiful rebel* is about that sort of custodial role. Its finale presents the union of its protagonists as a model for the compromises that will make possible the fact of Canada. In the moral and symbolic languages we have been observing, the universal applicability of specific facts is taken as a given. The warning tone, the prophetic strain, the scriptural figures of speech, stem from a common confidence in the significance of a culture's doings. Differences may occur as to the exact nature of the significance, but no one denies a peculiar importance to the processes examined. This ability to generalize, however, falters as the century proceeds.

III

A beautiful rebel spoke for a culture in which romantic idealism was already losing its capacity for bending history to its will. The attempt to create a heroic past for a pragmatic present succeeded only in underlining the distance between the two. That gap grew too large to ignore. The question it posed was a vexing one: how can a culture retain a heritage when the romantic, heroic, and idealistic speech that grants it significance has grown obsolete in public discourse? The answer lay in putting an emphasis on the hardship and struggle of pioneer life alongside a preoccupation with the technics employed by the pioneers. As realism came to overpower romance in historical fiction, textbooks and popular fiction began to reflect what I call an Upper Canada Village approach to the Loyalist past.

The shift in historical fiction can be illustrated through two novels. The first, Ralph Connor's *The runner* (1929), uses an improbable hero, but places him in a likely setting. René la Flamme performs breathtaking feats with sword and pistol, but his costumed derring-do happens in a real Upper Canada, rife with injustice. The novel is as much about 1837 as about 1812. It takes no less a figure than Brock to deliver to René the statist exhortations that will take his mind off his rage over crooked land deals: ' "You are nothing! I am nothing! Our country, sir, is all!"'[19] The 'fervently patriotic, savagely anti-American' Loyalists, themselves of purer patriotic strain than the Late Loyalists, triumph over the unwitting quislings of the peace party. Here social violence, as in Tennyson's *Maud*, deftly solves problems both narrative and political.

The second novel, Maida Parlow French's *Boughs bend over* (1943), along with its sequel, *All this to keep* (1947), makes it clear that realism has now become the accepted way of telling the Loyalist story. These chronicles of the Van Doorn family's fortunes in Upper Canada are set until their very end in the struggle-filled years before 1812. Thus they bypass the glamour and excitement of the miltary period. Strongly matriarchal in outlook, the series (written by a UEL descendant) sticks to the mundane matters of poverty in exile, troublesome relatives, price-gouging, land-stealing speculators, and the pains of love. Like many UELs in reality but none else in fiction, the Van Doorns are not of British origin. They are not colonized in their hearts, and therefore display a certain scepticism toward the motives of the motherland. Simcoe remains for them 'a British Empire autocrat,' while one of the villains is a half-pay officer who scorns his colonial charges and uses his position to cheat them.[20] Strong in their sense of communal and familial values, the novels present models of quiet and unassuming heroism. They convey the quality of early Upper Canadian life by dwelling upon such necessities as land clearing, farming, and milling. In doing this, they touch upon two Loyalist motifs that appear elsewhere. A passage in *Boughs bend over* pays close attention to the gathering of potash and to soap making, recalling C.W. Jefferys' icon of a pioneer woman at this task, while an incident in the story – a starving child eats a potato peeling planted as a seed during the Hungry Year and incurs the wrath of his parent – is based upon an anecdote appearing in Colonel Denison's previously mentioned article on the Loyalists.[21] Though the plot of the novel harbours some melodramatic elements (the evil miller seeking to foreclose on his neighbours, the missing title-deeds found in a secret place in the mill), they merely move the plot along through the daily round of labour and the issues of domestic economy. Even though two recent children's stories, Mary Alice and John Downie's *Honour bound* (1971) and Mary B. Fryer's *Escape: adventures of a Loyalist family* (1976), feature exciting chases through the wilderness until the promised land has been reached, both maintain a sure hold on family dynamics and the problems of accepting the duties brought by maturity. Of course, such themes form the stock-in-trade of most books found on the shelf marked Young People's Fiction. The relevance of these two to my argument is that they impose this same sort of 'realistic' and quotidian view of experience upon Loyalist families in flight from wrathful rebels. They do not, as they might have in the past, dwell solely upon hairbreadth escapes.

A certain realism in assessing the Loyalists' plight and a concentration upon the minutiae of pioneer labours sums up the treatment of Loyalism in post-World War II history textbooks in Ontario. For example, A.R.M. Lower and J.W. Chafe, *Canada – a nation and how it came to be* (1948), explicitly recounts the pains and penalties visited upon the Loyalists, yet avoids moralizing on this theme.[22] Instead, the authors hypothesize a situation in which an individual, forced to choose between one side and the other, naturally comes down on the side chosen by his neighbours and associates. This removes the discussion from the ideological heights it once occupied. Later texts, such as J.M.S. Careless' *Canada: a story of challenge* (1953) and Luella B. Creighton's *Canada: the struggle for empire* (1960), deal also in a realistic fashion with the business of political allegiance. George E. Tait's *Fair domain* (1960) devotes most of its space to a consideration of the techniques of agriculture, lumbering, and household economy at the time. The same is true of social science readers and junior texts, though it is fair to point out that at least one of the junior-high works comes up with a kind of flabby, vague, smiling-through discourse so typical of educationese. The statement that the Loyalists 'met the problems and hardships of pioneer life with cheerfulness and perseverance, and their example shone like a beacon for all who followed' merely repeats a present-day version of the genteel pieties found in the works of Stewart Wallace.[23]

Of course, earlier works intended for 'outside reading' in the schools covered the minutiae of pioneering as well, but their very titles indicated that they were concerned with these details rather than with the sweep of Canadian history.[24] The reader of the textbooks of our times comes across many more references to blacksmiths' forges than to the Queen's Rangers. The former, rather than the latter, appear as the key to understanding the Loyalist experience.

This pragmatic realism demonstrates how easily a sense of the Loyalist heritage might be obliterated by the forces of cultural change. To most schoolchildren and the general public, the Loyalists seem pioneers with a political grievance and not refugees from an unjust power who shored up a royalist levee on a continent nearly drowned in republicanism. Whereas the Loyalist experience can be used to bring into focus a number of issues – the 'totalist' aspect of revolutionary ideologies, the nature of political allegiance, the question of civil liberties for a group viewed with abhorrence by the majority, the dynamics of imperial states, and their treatment of settler minorities – its relevance is squeezed down to a concern with pioneering development and vestigial anti-Americanism. This stretches a broad, all-Canadian consensus over our varied regional experiences. Upper Canadians and Ukrainians in prairie sod huts come to stand for the same things, at whatever cost to the uniqueness of each.

Indeed, there are views even broader than the one that we are all pioneers together. A number of post-1945 history textbooks, riding the same wave of continentalist goodwill that from 1936 to 1945 produced the series sponsored by the Carnegie Endowment on Canadian-American joint occupancy of the continent, tended to leave the Loyalists out of the history of North America, the western hemisphere, or whatever vast extent of the globe the texts survey.²⁵ *North America and the modern world* (1947), *Canada and the Americas* (1953), and *Canada in the world today* (1954) have little to relate about the Loyalists that would excite any sense of historical grievance. Paring away the pieties of one generation need not dissolve the issues raised by a historical experience, yet this is what has happened. In an age swept by the terrors of ideological conflict, the one that founded anglophone Canada is tucked sideways into a log cabin and there thoroughly domesticated.

IV

Of course, the old élitism has gone with the romance, and that is no bad thing.²⁶ One must now return to *A beautiful rebel* or such popular histories as J. Castell Hopkins' *The story of Canada* (1902) and Roberts' *A history of Canada* to encounter a treatment of the UEL as best and brightest. The sale of Loyalist bric-à-brac (bronze plaques to serve either as door decorations or grave markers) may be announced in the *Globe and Mail*'s society column, but when Loyalists are mentioned in Peter Newman's calendar of success, *The Canadian establishment*, it is only to announce that one of their earliest settlements, Long Point, now contains an exclusive duck-hunting club populated largely by American millionaires. In 1866, the government of Canada West leased it to them in perpetuity, and there it stands, fenced off from the small provincial park that represents the public's hold on Long Point.²⁷

The movement from the moral / romantic to the realist / pragmatic involved a number of contradictions and ambiguities. A distinctive mark of a regional culture has been mixed in with a continental experience that has diluted it sufficiently to keep intact the homogeneous image of anglophone North America. The myth of pioneering is a heroic one that knows few ethnic boundaries. It is a safe one to exploit in a multicultural society, though it subtly promotes an evasion of the grittiness of historical experience. The fact that we are not what we once were comes to stand as a mark of honour, a badge of cultural superiority. A people who will not learn from history are not necessarily doomed to repeat it. They may instead forget it, and come to a shallow view of themselves and their potential.

In light of the process this chapter has decribed, we can better understand the desperate idealization of experience that shapes Jalna. The series represents the feeble and final stand of a view of Upper Canada that preserved its unique character, but only at the price of sentimentalization and the adoption of a vocabulary of experience wholly out of tune with its time. Thus Jalna's message involved a mummification of realities never as universal or concrete as the series held them to be. Here stood a ripple rather than a counter-current to the stronger drift of events. Both processes proved congenial to each other. After all, the de-moralizing and homogenizing of the Loyalist experience could proceed apace while imaginative allegiance was still accorded to a structure too far from reality ever to shape it.

Interlude: *A New Athens*

Just as *A beautiful rebel* summed up an earlier way of coming to terms with the Loyalist fact, so Hugh Hood's *A new Athens* (Ottawa: Oberon 1977) denotes a current mode of understanding a culture's sense of its own roots. The structures of the imagination can supply continuity where history proclaims disruption. This novel, the second in a projected twelve-volume *roman-fleuve* on Canada in the twentieth century, depicts a heritage existing largely in museums, yet one which somehow continues to offer a model of experience for the lives of its characters. The implications are ambiguous, however, in that a portion of the heritage remains in a cultural attic while some aspects of it live on in social habits. The visionary imagination forming the core of the book incorporates the Loyalist theme into its final tapestry of Upper Canada/Ontario.

A more serious work of fiction than any of Mazo de la Roche, the novel has certain resemblances to her work in its sense of Ontario life as a procession of continuity and change. Though Hood evokes the Loyalist fact in greater scope and explicitness than de la Roche, he employs it as one of a number of causes of the cultural weightiness of Upper Canada over the decades. The ideas of the gentry, the myth of the covenant, the sense of a social and moral élite: these do not particularly concern the novel. Its narrator, Matt Goderich, follows the practices of a romantic poet and subordinates all 'outside' experience to the categories of the human imagination, whether his own or that of others. Thus the three climactic moments in the novel are visionary: the narrator's initial recollection of the significance of an abandoned railway cutting he stumbles upon, his later discovery of a sunken ship even as he is falling in love, and his final recognition of the power of a visionary artist.† The

† Hood, *A new Athens*, 18–20, 112–14, 209–16.

Loyalist fact in this work functions as another of the narrative, descriptive motifs shaping the hero's Wordsworthian, mystical responses to reality. In a world held together by the narrator's synthetic powers, the Loyalist heritage becomes an aspect of an Upper Canadian culture whose seamlessness provides a solid ground for his visions of unity.

If Loyalism and its accompanying attitudes towards culture and society remain a motif rather than a central concern of *A new Athens*, they add a rich particularity to the story.† Its title provides images of both cultural renewal and preservation. Renewal is associated with the apocalyptic Athens of Shelley in the final chorus of *Hellas*, where the world's great age begins anew and another Athens arises; Athens figures again, this time in *Prometheus unbound*, as an apocalyptic city, since the liberated Titan and his love, Asia, take up their abode within a sacred grove nearby. New World, new Adam, new Athens: the boundless promise of the continent reveals itself here. Preservation, the continuance and extension of the nobler traditions of the Old World, also is linked with the name of Athens in a statement made by Matt. Where he once considered pretentious the changing of Farmersville's name to Athens (on the grounds that it had two schools), he now sees that 'what they had done wasn't to insinuate that their village was as great, as central to culture as the city of Athena, but only that their schools were in the tradition of the Academy, that human culture is continuous, that a Canadian school two generations removed from the wilderness is the same kind of school as the Academy, that human nature persists, remains self-identical through many generations of superficial changes' (59). Similarly, Loyalism and its survivals offer another model of a seamless culture and an enduring human nature.

Much is made of the Loyalist origins of Stoverville (Hood's mythical Brockville.)‡ The town's élite still occupy the waterfront properties awarded to Loyalist officers. Matt's rise in his profession as art historian comes with the success of his monograph, *Stone dwellings of Loyalist country*. At one point, in discussing an aspect of the town's history, the narrator discloses how historical fact offers a parallel structure for personal choice. He is commenting on the Loyalist effort of 1812 and the dawning realization that the covenant might not loom as hugely in imperial interests as it did in Upper Canada's. The wary defence of the St Lawrence by the empire's gunboats and the construction of the Rideau Canal system, capped by the final development

† By Loyalism as a motif, I mean a) the explicit use of Loyalism as a historical fact, and b) the use of the displaced Loyalist myth observed in the Jalna series, a social mythology emphasizing stability and endurance whose origins lie in Loyalism.

‡ Further comments on this aspect of the novel appear in my '*A new Athens*, the new Jerusalem, a new Atlantis,' *Fiddlehead* no. 117 (spring 1978): 105.

of the east-west railway, meant that Upper Canada was becoming Ontario and looking north rather than towards the river. He concludes with a historical and yet private summation: 'When Edie and I turned away from the riverfront that she loved and I admired, to build our summer cottage on an inland lake near Athens, we were recapitulating, perhaps without being fully aware of it – the constitutive, essential story of life in the colony which became Ontario. Life along the river was enchantingly beautiful and easy, but dangerous, expensive, likely to deliver us from one moment to the next into the hands of unwanted masters' (185).

The analogy between the couple and the colony may be strained, but it does demonstrate how a set of historical facts can be used to tell a contemporary story. Matt discovers a sunken gunboat from the days when the Canadian shore needed to be safeguarded from American pirates. The boat is now a museum piece; a number of Upper Canadian villages stand either in the same state or rot as instant Atlantises beneath the St Lawrence Seaway. In fact, the pirates did not board us, we joined them. Of course, that pessimistic a reading of the facts falls outside this novel, and the boat's rescue is more properly interpreted as a recovery of a culture presumed dead. The ship appears as an emblem stating that the drowned villages along the seaway exist at least in part in Upper Canada Village. The preceding chapter outlined the extent to which such a gesture reduces the relevance of the Loyalist heritage to one of pioneering alone. This is not quite the case with the British ark, though there is enough of an 'olden days' air about it to mark the vessel off firmly from the concerns of the present. Yet its rudder surfaces as a marker in a townswoman's garden. The heritage is mixed, of varying degrees of relevance.

To recapitulate, however, the novel is permeated with historical fact and consequence. One character's last name is Boston. Adamses abound, both as American revolutionaries and as archetypal American Adams. Such facts of the Canadian experience as Loyalism, British North America, the presence of the USA, and the persistence of these facts in the characters' lives present a set of motifs attesting to the weight of history within a culture.

Since the novel refuses to budge from the pastoral mode, even its concern with matters of money and social class (see especially 159–60) cannot squeeze out of the book the defensive and fearful tone found in other writers to be viewed in the next chapter. One reviewer deplores what he sees as the novel's unwarranted optimism, but what interests this study is that Loyalism gets brought under observation as a set of personal beliefs and habits, though no longer as a prime mover of the Upper Canadian historical experience.† It

† See Sam Solecki, 'Metafiction or metahistory,' *Canadian Forum* LVII (Dec.–Jan. 1977–8): 105.

functions instead as one of a number of agents producing an enduring culture, and much of that culture goes on inside someone's head. Hood's use of the Loyalist past indicates in fact how passé that cultural fact has become.

The assertive, defensive stance of Mazo de la Roche exists no longer. No prophet cries that an imperilled way of life must be preserved. Christian apologists used the old gods as decorative and allegorical figures, while post-Christian writers scatter Christ figures through their work as a way of heightening their secularist heroes. For Hood the Loyalist motif works like that gunboat in the museum. A force that once defended and shaped a culture survives only as a dimly perceived and oblique determinant of the present. A less sunny pastoral might turn this sense of loss into anguished reflection rather than implicit observation. Instead, history's terror and chaos are subordinated to a vision of its evolutionary fulfilment. If the writers in the next chapter seem Catastrophist in the theory of the progress of Canadian society, with change brought about through a succession of cataclysms, then Hood appears as a uniformitarian who concentrates on the accretion of minute changes rather than on spectacular shifts in consciousness. The new Athens, perched between rock and river, holds within its space an array of gorgeous and well-preserved fossils. One of them is Loyalism.

Loyalism therefore figures within a pluralistic vision of the sources of Ontario's culture. The heavenly city seen in the visionary art which Matt beholds near the end of the novel accommodates all terrestrial themes and realities into its larger pattern of experience. Loyalism dwells not only within that ultimate framework, functioning as one of a set of historical factors. Centrality denied, existence affirmed; primacy ignored, plurality hailed; survival replaces triumph: here then is the limit of endurance, the final classification of a cultural beginning and the announcement of an end.

7 The Ancestral Present

Loving memories constitute an indispensable psychological resource in maturity ... The belief that in some ways the past was a happier time by no means rests upon a sentimental illusion; nor does it lead to a backward-looking, reactionary paralysis of the political will – Christopher Lasch, *The culture of narcissism* (New York 1979), 24–5

The most influential document on culture and its support this country produced could not avoid mentioning Loyalism early in the report. 'When the United Empire Loyalists came to British North America they were carried as communities through the years of danger and hardships by their faithful adherence to a common set of beliefs. Canada became a national entity because of certain habits of mind and convictions which its people shared and would not surrender. Our country was sustained through difficult times by the power of this legacy.'[1] The rhetoric of the Massey Report – as this quotation attests – repeated the usual Loyalist allusions to a spiritual inheritance and a covenantal fidelity to it. The Canada it addressed, however, the Canada whose culture it sought to preserve, had come upon difficult times that could not be attributed to widespread material hardship. These difficulties have not eased in the thirty years since the publication of that report. The equivalent of a spiritual inflationary factor has diminished the practical worth of the legacy. Yet 'certain habits of mind and convictions' never vanish without trace, even though the historical circumstances that produced them appear to belong on the other side of a vast continental – and continentalist – divide. This chapter therefore deals with a number of contemporary writers who display a set of preoccupations consistent with those we have previously examined. Shakespeare tells us that time hath a wallet at his back; among the alms for oblivion that pack contains are portions of the Loyalist legacy. We can discuss those pieces in a variety of ways, but in our time they are borne as tokens of sorrow, remembrances of Zion glimpsed from beside the waters of Babylon. Whether directly or only implicitly employed, the Loyalist myth now functions as a model of exile, discontinuity, and loss.

George Grant, Scott Symons, Dennis Lee, and Al Purdy reveal in varying degrees a sense of a world poorly lost. Their view of the state of man remains essentially one based upon the sense of a fall. The defeat of Loyalism and the kind of Canada it stood for presents one historical instance of a fall.† As is the case elsewhere in this book, I am tracing a habit of mind rather than a specific theory, so that this chapter deals with a common set of concerns rather than with an explicit ideology. Of course, the sense of a fall provides an enduring theme in human culture, and certainly a critic cannot ascribe this to neo-Loyalism. My argument, however, is that the particular interest these Ontario writers display in the idea of a fall links them with a local tradition of Loyalist concerns. Their writings at times deal specifically with Loyalist materials and Loyalism remains a vital factor among the many producing their particular stances. I say this, not to pigeonhole these figures, but to indicate how greatly a certain cultural attitude remains with us still.

I

In one of the best commentaries to appear on the writing of George Grant, R.D. MacDonald alludes to 'the pastoral myth which lies behind Grant's tragic vision, a pastoral myth which Grant and his readers must know has never been an actuality or even an agreed fiction in the Canadian setting.' In this version of pastoral, the critic continues, 'Adam stands not so much as an inhabitant of the Garden but as the dispossessed tenant, removed from a world which had manifested something sacred and timeless, living now in a new world of chaos which is contained, perhaps, in some shadowy and distant order.'[2] As MacDonald points out, the dystopian pastoral myth in *Lament for a nation* emerges as a description of the lot of fallen man in which the recollection of happiness heightens exilic anguish. Such feelings, theologians assure us, offer the sharpest of hell's tortures.

† The Americanization of Canada, while a major factor in that fall, cannot bear full responsibility for it. The decline of Britain's imperial power, the colonization of the west with its subsequent development of a regional identity, and the importance in the country of non-British and non-anglophone groups, whether as founding races or immigrants, were bound to weaken the sense of a covenantal relationship with Great Britain that lay at the heart of Loyalism and the national attitudes it fostered over the decades. Because anti-Americanism remains so widespread and 'legitimate' an attitude here, the death of Loyalist (i.e., *British* North American) Canada can conveniently be ascribed to the American takeover of the nation's economic life. My contention is the sale of this country merely hastened a process that was inevitable in view of the factors mentioned.

This usage – indirect and implicit – presents a sharp contrast to Hood's overt employment of Loyalism. With Grant we begin an exploration of writers who move into a new, 'inner' mode of Loyalist exile. Reducing Grant's rich and complex thought to a paradigm of the Loyalist mythology resembles arranging a Beethoven piano sonata for the banjo, but only by this means can the reader grasp the necessity for including him in this study. John Muggeridge's essay on Grant frequently invokes the term 'loyalist' in describing the author's attitudes, yet the piece shows how easily one can invoke 'the Loyalist tradition' without ever getting at its particulars.[3] My task here is to follow his thought in a dialectical rather than chronological form in order to place him within the tradition I have been examining.

Grant's writing delineates a mind firmly rooted in North America, sensitive to the grandeurs and miseries of that stance. He resists anyone attributing his distaste for post-1945 Canada to the fact of his ancestry.[4] Yet he himself points out his origins in a class whose 'ancestors had all been thrown out [of the USA],' noting that 'nothing so much can drive one to philosophy as being part of a class which is disappearing.'[5] If his Loyalist forbears gave him his 'deep ancestral antipathy to the United States,' they also planted in him a sense of the possibilities of the New World and the virtues of the peculiar Loyalist engraftment on to it.[6] 'In defence of North America' mentions 'the stringency and nobility of that primal encounter' between white settlers and an unmastered continent. However obsessed we may be at present with the price of that mastery, the author cannot ignore 'what was necessary and what was heroic in that conquest.'[7] Through it, North America became 'the first continent called to bring human excellence to birth throughout the whole range of the technological society.'[8]

British North America in its heyday answered that call (note the religious overtones of that term) when it at once grappled with the tests of this continent and still maintained its vital ties with the western, British traditions that had brought it into being. 'Precarious,' 'ambiguous,' 'dividedly poised' are the terms Grant uses to describe nineteenth-century Canada as a complex dual monarchy of the spirit in which the claims both of Britain and North America would be reconciled.[9] 'To be a Canadian was to be a unique species of North American.'[10]

A complex and bracing fate, to have been a Canadian, and the fall reduced complexity to opposition. Strangely, the degenerative process began with the birth of Loyalism during the American Revolution, for the exiles bore with them the seeds that would choke their harvest. Grant does not offer us a single dramatic event that produced the fall, though *Lament* locates in the fate of John Diefenbaker a conclusive reminder that Canada had fallen. In fact, even to conceive of Canada's fall was to adopt a desperate position: 'To most Canadians, the existence of our society is so right, so true, that it is unthinkable that it should be swallowed up or destroyed.'[11] Yet destroyed it was, or rather it was split in two, with its British traditions no longer able to pose a counterweight to its American ones.

In his vision of Fall as Split, Grant resembles a number of other cultural theorists – all of them of a specifically religious orientation in both their lives and writings – but he has applied their sense of degeneration to the fact of English Canada.[12] Canada split because it could no longer balance its dual allegiance, its role in North America with its British origins. By denying the transatlantic authority, it fell under the total sway of the other. Continental drift in North America guaranteed that any nation here without a double allegiance would pay for its simplicity by subjection to the United States. In a passage that could pass as screened autobiography, Grant recalls the onset of what he had previously described as the unthinkable: 'Plato came of a family which for generations had helped to shape Athens in its glory. Yet he reached maturity just as the results of the Peloponnesian War became catastrophically clear both for Athens and its enemies.'[13] The enemies of the new Athens were not merely the Liberal party, not even its allies in an Americanized ruling class, not even the might of the American empire itself, though all these monsters stalk the pages of *Lament* and other writings. The true foes are the forces of modernity, the drives which place North America in the vanguard of technological civilization.

The Loyalists' descendants have now lost the new kingdom given their ancestors after their exodus from the old. The war in our time resembles the earlier one, in that the battle was lost to our own countrymen, the Liberal/liberal Canada that achieved its victory with the fall of the Diefenbaker remnant in 1963. This did not occur through weakness and treachery alone. Just as imperial Britain itself produced the Whig revolutionary tradition that gave the rebel Americans an ideology, so the British traditions in Loyalism generated the homogenizing forces that would eventually negate the possibility of Canada. The Loyalists themselves, children of the age of progress, would plant firmly in Canadian soil the anti-particularist principles of modernity. A culture's complexity would shrink into ambiguity (*Lament*, 63–8).

Grant's argument frequently employs the concept of loyalty, though that becomes a matter of allegiance to residual rather than to still vital traditions. It is the habit of mind characteristic of those 'of deep loyalty, who found themselves impotent in the face of their disappearing past' (*Lament*, 33). For in its intellectual forbears, Hume and Locke, English Canada provided the ancestors for its executioners.[14]

The very language in which the covenant was cast destined its rupture. The pragmatic, modernist assumptions of English political philosophy could no more withstand the enemies of the kind of Canada that Loyalism stood for than could the administration of Lord North the critics of the American war. And, as if these forces were not enough (I admit the considerable philosophical question-begging in an account such as mine), the energies of the horizonless world of modernity that Nietzsche foresaw would devastate the fact of Canada.

However remote *Also sprach Zarathustra* seems from the determinedly pragmatic culture of English Canada, Grant's CBC Massey Lectures, *Time as history* (1969), demonstrate its proximity. The German thinker realized that the death of the Christian God erased even more than the intellectual and cultural horizon that had given birth to the west. If the historicism that accompanied God's death discerned the arbitrary nature of the horizons beheld by any and all cultures, then all future horizons would also attain the status of nothing more than conventionalized stage sets. The result – and we now turn back to Canada – of this newly flattened earth compels the disappearance of particularity and the subordination of local affections and moralities to the universal, homogenizing pursuit of appetite and mastery.[15] A year before the appearance of *Lament*, Grant was to write that 'as modern people came to believe themselves to be the absolute source of themselves, all systems of order and meaning which appear to human beings as myth became other to them, and so in the very act of their sovereignty they experience the world as empty of meaning.'[16] What resistance therefore can a modernized citizenry like Canada's offer to the drives of its powerful neighbour, when those drives are the homogenizing ones of modernity itself?

Though cast out from their first home, the Loyalists found a refuge to the north and made a garden there. This political alternative of a world elsewhere disappears in the face of the sort of eviction Grant describes. Well, what then of the mind, the imagination, the soul? What of those shelters? Here Grant disappoints those who would assert that even to recognize the wilderness as wilderness implies that somewhere there must be a garden. In trying times, he has written, men often seek refuge in the certainties of the past. 'Such reactionary experiments are always vain.'[17] As a philosopher strongly aware of the uses of philology, one sensitive enough to the role played by language in the definition of political realities to entitle a work *English-speaking justice*, he holds that language itself rebuts our attempt to derive from our experience of deprivation some plan for reconstructing a new/old world of the good.[18] As his explorations into the nature of modernity itself argue, it is as if the Loyalists, cast out of one land, found that their swords could never be turned into plowshares for shaping the other.

Plato provides us with an instructive image here. Since we are born in the cave and die there as well, we cannot fully sense the sunlight our more gifted brethren claim to have experienced. For Grant, modernity forms a cave within the cave that is life on this earth. We remain at such a distance from those suns we describe as Athens and Jerusalem that we cannot recognize the nature and extent of the gap. The inescapability of our culture's solipsism forms a motif in Grant's writing. As he remarks in one of his most profound works:

But the goal of modern striving – the building of free and equal human beings – leads inevitably back to a trust in the expansion of that very technology we are attempting to judge. The unfolding of modern society has not only required the criticism of all older standards of human excellence, but has also at its heart that trust in the overcoming of chance which leads us back to judge every human situation as being solvable in terms of technology. As moderns we have no standards by which to judge particular techniques, except standards welling up with our faith in technical expansion.[19]

The Grant *persona* has changed from that of exile to wanderer, his life an itinerary whose stopping points come at those grace-filled moments when the Good reveals itself. 'An impotent stranger in the practical realm of one's own society,' the individual who discovers the extent of his alienation from that community may have made 'a necessary discovery, but it is always an emasculating one.'[20] The stark, sexual images bring home to the reader the sincerity of the anguished remark that 'it is a terrible moment for the individual when he crosses the Rubicon and puts that faith [in "unlimited technological development"] into question.'[21] The Rubicon's appearance in an essay on the fate of Canada reminds us that Grant has conflated a number of sources and images in his account of cultural fall, and that he sees Canada's fate in the light of the progress and destiny of the west. Yet his framework for apprehending the Canadian experience remains one of fall and exile at the hands of one's own countrymen. Here is the Loyalist pattern repeated. Pause here, along another classical riverbank, the Virgilian shore that Grant occupies in his conclusion to *Lament*. The spirits of the dead in the *Aeneid*, like Canadians exiled from a world they thought they knew and believed they occupied, extend to their visitors a gesture of yearning as they depart: 'They were holding their arms outstretched in love toward the further shore.'[22] The image of the stream begins to flood as it encompasses the Jordan and the waters of Babylon; all streams seek the ocean for their final rest. Along these currents the Loyalist exile must voyage, through 'an age of clouded night.'[23]

II

Grant wrote an enthusiastic introduction to Scott Symons' *Heritage*, while Dennis Lee serves as one of the dedicatees for both *Technology and empire* and *English-speaking justice*. Lee's critical work, *Savage fields*, acknowledges its debt to Grant, and the poet opens *Civil elegies* with an epigraph from the philosopher.[24] Some community of sentiment and like-mindedness may be deduced from this. Though it does some disservice to Symons the novelist and Lee the poet to deal with them as if they embodied a different aspect of Grant's concerns, some analytical benefit can be gained. Briefly, Symons incorporates the explicitly Loyalist and imperialist Grant in so far as the novelist chronicles the loss involved in Canada's severance of its ties with a larger communion. Lee, in his philosophic estrangement, parallels the plight of Symons as a cultural exile. He also illustrates the other side of Grant, in that the movement in Lee's writing from *Civil elegies* to *Savage fields* draws out a critical theory based on alienation that is first proclaimed in a series of poems offering public laments in the fashion of Grant. Both Symons and Lee merit attention in themselves, but viewing them from the perspective established here links them in a common intimation of the state of English Canada and the exile into which some of its spirits have ventured.

III

The sheer aridity of the public world will indeed drive many to such excellence in strange and dangerous kingdoms (as those of drugs and myth and sexuality). In such kingdoms, moderation and courage may be known by the wise to be essential virtues. But when such virtues have been publicly lost they cannot be inculcated by incantation, but only rediscovered in the heat of life where many sparrows fall. Much suffering will be incurred by those who with noble intent follow false trails. Who is to recount how and when and where private anguish and public catastrophe may lead men to renew the vision of excellence?[25]

Everywhere I go in Canada, I find people deprived of their traditional values and beliefs. I find a people cowering behind their loss of history.[26]

Out of that sense of deprivation ('private anguish and public catastrophe') summed up by Grant, Symons began the journey that convinced him of a nationwide state of shock. His myth of English Canadian society, with which he has fused a personal myth of enlightenment and prophetic mission, recounts a fall from Tory-Anglican-Loyalist integration into the split, smug, sexually circumscribed world of 'Methodism-cum-modernism.' The gap between the two can now be bridged only by a sexual openness, especially in an emerging male homosexuality. This return to a world of touch offers the sole hope for the resurrection of a sacramental world in which real objects contain their spiritual aspects and man exists harmoniously within a tactile-symbolic universe.

The blend of Tory Loyalism and Gay Liberation makes Symons' myth one of the more eclectic in our intellectual history. On its own terms, the belief is a coherent one, with an enormous appetite for widely disparate phenomena that get subsumed finally within a theological vocabulary. The uses to which the Loyalist myth can still be put, the endurance of the habits of mind it produces, serve as lessons to be learned from Symons' work.

Up to and including Mazo de la Roche, the writers studied imagined Loyalism in terms of covenant and reciprocal fidelity. The writers in this chapter view it in terms of fall and exile. Grant's implict dystopian pastoral, where a once-coherent society reveals itself only through painfully beheld fragments, becomes far more explicit in the writings of Symons. Through a process of polemical conflation the Loyalist garden attains its most luxuriant growth in the Rosedale of the author's boyhood, though the 'ongoing garden party' lives now merely in memory.[27]

The idea of fall as split which Grant shares with other theorists occurs in Symons. Once again, the fall is seen to have come about when our culture split its senses from its intellect. Symons, however, does not locate this moment, as have others, during the Renaissance. Instead, he moves the dates up, presenting a view of Loyalist Canada as an integrated, almost pre-modern culture, a view that philosophical investigation cannot support. What is in Grant a sense of tragic complexity then declines here into polemic. Grant realizes that the Loyalists, as Americans and heirs to the age of progress, brought with them the seeds of rationalism and pragmatism that, full-grown, would choke the flowering of their Canadian garden. This ironic complexity, Symons denies. The Loyalists instead suffer from an imported virus, and thus their artefacts are described in before-the-fall terms: 'In 1800, and right on into living memory, culture, quality, physical creativity – these lived together in Canada. Meditation with the hands, and touch with the mind, were not separated in any significant way.'[28] If the reader shrugs at the construction of a high-rise of doctrine atop a marsh of assertive rhetoric, he also notes the acuity of Symons' points about the cultured nature of the Loyalist experience. The textbook sleight-of-hand by which Loyalism equals pioneering, the log-cabin view of the settlement of Upper Canada, the smug acceptance of an image of spiritual poverty: these get their come-uppance at his hands. 'Starting right from scratch on the land, these Loyalists were not starting from scratch in themselves – either spiritually, emotionally, or culturally. They retained not only their experience of living in America, but also the fundamental elements of an Anglo-Saxon civilization a thousand years old ... ' 'A people poor but proud. A people living in peasant conditions – yet part of a princely culture.'[29] Observe the final sentence fragments. Symons does not fall into the error of overcompensation, he does not present us with ladies and gents in ball gowns and knee-breeches assembling at Dundurn Castle as they alight from bateaux. The squirarchical aspect of his Loyalist myth does not appear until his recital of bygone Rosedale glories. He calls attention to those elegancies only because they have degenerated into 'merely money-with-manners.'[30] The author's perspective contains a very long fall, a progressive shrinking of unified sensibilities first into élite enclaves (Rosedale; the Hamilton viewed as central to Christian Loyalism) until even those bastions crumbled.[31] One seeks in vain for precision in these matters, but the general drift of the myth places the fall in the triumph of a non-sacramental Protestantism. Thoroughly pragmatic and non-contemplative, it split spirit from body and came to govern the nation's public and commercial life.

Who then brought about that split? Symons' arraignment of public enemies entails considerable labelling. The 'mute mediocre Methodist mannikin' of a 1963 speech has by the time of *Place d'Armes* (1967) become the 'Cube' and the ECM ('Emancipated Canadian Methodist'). By 1969 and *Civic square* we have the 'Blandman,' citizen of 'McCanadaland,' one of the 'Smugly Fucklings.'[32] To this host of foes – no one list ever quite encompasses them all – he finally pens a hymn of hate that acknowledges their power and purposefulness:

The Methodists would rule
Did the Empire have to be turned upside down
    they would rule
Did Authority have to be subverted
    they would rule

Did the Crown have to be betrayed
    they would rule

And it would be a Good State for the Nicest People
Tyranny of Respectabilitude[33]

De la Roche receives favourable mention in *Civic square* (216). To her sense of familial rootedness (which some would call snobbery), Symons adds a bitterness that springs from a sense of defeat. In a rigged conversation that could have jumped out of the pages of one of his novels, he and the owner of a fireplace he is studying exchange a conspiracy theory: ' "This mantle ... it's really a whole style of life, Donald. And in our time, it has not merely been replaced, it has been systematically destroyed ... hasn't it?" I ask. " ... Yes Scott ... we have been systematically destroyed." '[34]

The lineaments of the myth encountered in Grant (the fall/split at the hands of a modernizing element in Canadian society, the total nature of the defeat) shine forth here without Grant's intellectual sophistication and discrimination. Nor do they carry his stylistic weight. The tincture of rage and bitterness in Symons' work limits the ideas' attractiveness. The obsessional polemic closes the two novels in upon themselves until the pasteboard characters of *Place d'Armes* recede into the near-total self-absorption in *Civic square*. Even when the ideology has been largely dissipated (as in an excerpt from a work in progress, *Helmet of flesh*), and the usual content and setting shifted (an encounter with an elemental, stylish sheikh in darkest Morocco), the narrator's concerns remain firmly 'inner.'[35]

If the works do not stand out as novels (and it is fair to add that the author has repeatedly expressed his wish to be taken as someone other than a novelist, as a subtitle to *Place d'Armes*, 'A combat journal,' indicates), a glance at one of the difficulties with their message throws light on exactly how they ought to be classified. Their version of Loyalism as Anglicanism flies in the face of at least two large historical facts: 1)the large number of Loyalists of the Dutch Reformed faith, chiefly from New York, among them the leader of the first band to land at the Bay of Quinte, Peter Van Alstyne; 2) the Congregational meeting-house structure of the earliest Loyalist churches in Upper Canada and the Maritimes. The pioneering historian of Upper Canadian Loyalism, Egerton Ryerson, had his differences with the Church of England. The Anglicanization of Loyalism seems to have happened well after its historical origins, as that faith came to stand for gentility and imperial ties. Loyalism's baptism by myth may be one of Strachan's gentler contributions to Canadian culture, but its appearance in Symons' narratives turns them into biased polemics.

In fact, his narratives resemble nothing so much as evangelical sermons from the saved to sinners who are brands to be plucked from the burning.[36] Everything in the books stays subordinate to their exhortative goals. Characters and incidents function as *exempla* for the doctrines expounded. The characters easily fall into Good and Evil categories. Thus greater individuality can be found in the pieces of furniture described in *Heritage* than among the various male prostitutes that parade through *Place d'Armes*.

The strange union of Anglican message and evangelical form recalls another kind of contradiction that occurs in the work of Walt Whitman, whose enterprise exhibits certain affinities with Symons'. The most self-consciously American of poets, who casually included an annexed Canada in his continental visions, proclaimed his love for anonymous, distant, or dead persons better than he portrayed the figures of those palpable and close at hand. The super-American Whitman and the anti-American Symons appear to be cousins in their prolixity, preachiness, homo-eroticism and yearning for love at a distance. Symons' blend of Yankee self-absorption and evangelical didacticism in fact places him closer to the actual Loyalists than to Loyalists of later, mythological versions. In his style and substance, he remains British North American, but with the initial word of the phrase not always the most definitive.

Is there balm in Gilead, or is Symons' sense of Canada's self-betrayal despairing? He finds an end to our fallen condition, not in the world of politics, but in the inner light of a sacramental religion. In keeping with his anti-Protestantism, he puts forward a doctrine of Real Presence as the key image of the properly integrated life.† That doctrine, a theoretical support for loyalism as Anglicanism, could be subscribed to only by Anglo-Catholics, never by the majority of Anglicans at any time. The sacramental retreat into a belief that has long since lost any social force offers a bourgeois, romantic solution, though Symons would probably not choose to label it as that. It also involves an excursion into French Canada, following *The golden dog* in its attempt to tie that culture into its knot of loyalty. The doctrine of the Real Presence is a Roman Catholic one. Therefore, since this doctrine implies for Symons an approach to experience that is integrated rather than split, that portion of Canada that remained (until recently) avowedly Roman Catholic must have maintained an organically integrated culture. This then is the image of Quebec presented in *Place d'Armes*.

Symons' success during his time as a journalist in discovering and

---

† The belief that the host consecrated at the Eucharist is changed in essence to the actual body and blood of Christ is metaphorically extended by Symons into an image of the oneness of human experience, especially of all sexual experience. There, human inner-ness and touch blend in the deepest fashion.

interpreting the Quiet Revolution for English Canada ought not to distract the reader from his ideology's affinities with the conservative, agrarian Quebec nationalism that the new doctrines were replacing. His Quebec of handicrafts and churches is more that of the Abbé Groulx than of Jean Lesage, which explains why his narrative can accommodate Place d'Armes but not Place Ville Marie. The conclusion of *Place d'Armes* shows the English Canadian hero dashing out of 'La Paroisse' with a sacred host in his hand as a token of the various communions (largely sexual) he has experienced. Such a gesture would only shock any bystander from the old Quebec and bewilder anyone from the new. George Grant has been quoted on the uselessness of snatching gestures from an earlier and alien tradition as a stylistic fillip for alienated moderns. Symons himself bears that out in writing that he and his friend 'have taken Rosedale, the *real* Rosedale with us ... We made Rosedale into a *Real* Presence, instead of a mere memory. It only cost us our lives.'[37] The concept grows a bit gamier in the opening of *Civic square*:

oh, just know that cocks like
cunts and
Christianity, are beautiful is all
you need to know

is absolutely all ...[38]

Both statements resemble quasi-Metaphysical conceits rather than reliable poultices for the ache of modernity. Like the flaming, crucified penises with which the author decorated the limited-edition printing of *Civic square*, their shock value only temporarily distracts the reader from the fact that no single image or term can support so heavy a weight of meaning.

To turn from bogus sacramentalism to a book like *Heritage* is to discover a Symons far more authentic, one who remains content to describe a paradise lost rather than come up with a nostrum for regaining it. The reader need not hold that pre-confederation furniture represents the last link we possess with a world before the fall to delight in Symons' powers as a polemicist and his sensitivity as a connoisseur. The unabashedly partisan, sensuous, and joyful tone of the book lifts it above an antique-buyer's manual and thrusts it toward the status of a Canadian *Stones of Venice*. In *Heritage*, the Loyalist pattern of experience has swung full circle, with the initial rage at dispossession transformed into a view from across the gulf at a glory that once was. Symons recalls the stance assumed by Grant when his finest work leaves the reader with the glimpse of a figure stretching out his hands, with love, from a further shore.

IV

A new Athens employs Ontario's Loyalist past in the way a writer on contemporary Manitoba might incorporate the vestigial remains of the Red River Settlement. To Grant and Symons Loyalism gives an image for their contemporary experience which fixes patterns of dispossession and exile in an audience's mind. Though philosopher and novelist–higher-journalist (the role Symons best plays) need not be equated, they indicate how a kind of fall-out from the Loyalist catastrophe (for current 'Loyalists' stress the fall rather than the garden) remains at work in the bones of Upper Canadian intellectual life.[39]

The next two writers, Dennis Lee and Al Purdy, do not deal with a specifically Loyalist myth of dispossession. Still, the specific shapes they give to their treatment of exile and alienation owe something to the cultural context we have been examining. To attribute the *angst* their work exhibits to Loyalism alone would resemble viewing Kafka solely as a product of the fall of the Hapsburg empire. Just as a pattern of experience in the Jalna series links it with themes concerned with Loyalism, so we may find in the pain recorded by Lee and Purdy some kinship with Grant and Symons.

Lee's '1838' and 'When I Went Up to Rosedale' (*The gods*) present a diptych of failed Canadas. On the one hand, the republican Canada of William Lyon Mackenzie, choked at birth and now offering a dubious nationalist prototype, since a republic could have been even more easily Americanized than the alternative that prevailed; on the other, a pretentious colonial mediocrity that aped grandeur as a means of legitimizing unearned privilege. Loyalism and Mackenzie do not mix, yet Lee rightly belongs here on account of his vision of a fallen Canada, though his version of history may not agree with Symons'. The eighth stanza of 'Rosedale' conveys the dilemma experienced by anyone trying to create a distinct, un-American Canada without re-inventing a lost Tory one:

> The dream of Tory origins
> Is full of lies and blanks,
> Though what remains when it is gone
> To prove that we're not Yanks?[40]

Neither the 'manic' nor the 'courtly' streets satisfy the poet's search for a real Canada, and it is the sense of loss that stamps the two poems.

To begin a consideration of a poet of Lee's stature by noticing two jingly works is not as irrelevant as it seems. The success of his children's verse points out one of his strongest gifts, that of simplicity, clarity, and cadence in the service of an often uncommon message. The two poems are songs rather than jingles, sprightly and trenchant summations of our present discontents. Indeed, 'Rosedale' catapults us into Lee's characteristic preoccupation, the nature of Canadian space and the relation between it and its occupants. This study has paused repeatedly at demarcated spaces, whether gardens, forests, estates, or national boundaries. Symons especially, with his geographically titled prose narratives, brings home to us this shared concern of the writers examined. His Rosedale is no less lost than Lee's, though the latter goes to it as a tourist rather than a native. How can the space that is Rosedale be reclaimed? It cannot simply be shut off, abandoned, ignored, even if it has been sold to the highest and nearest bidder. If it embodies, however wretchedly, our attempt to combine an older tradition with our North American one, then how can one gather from that garden of Klingsor without succumbing to its spell?

The year 1972 saw the appearance of *Civil elegies* and of what is almost a gloss on that volume, the article on 'Cadence, country, silence.' Lee not only acknowledged his debt to Grant in the article, as we have seen, but expressed his problems as an artist by using the spatial terminology that would form the mode of discourse in *Civil elegies*. If the task of Canadian artists compelled them 'not to fake a space of our own and write it up, but rather to find words for our space-lessness,' then the sequence of public verses sought to describe feelingly the emptiness of contemporary space here.[41]

To make much of nothing, to celebrate absence and the unrealized (as in Frost's 'The Road Not Taken'), is as characteristic a theme of modernist verse as the public announcement that the public world has vanished. A work such as Eliot's *The waste land* offers in its opening section one of the more memorable treatments of urban life in this century, with its vision of an unreal city thronged with spectral commuters tramping across a London Bridge that has fallen spiritually. London's neighbourhoods, sights, and smells abound in the poem, as they will later in the meditative *Four quartets*. Critical practice may have straitened the audience into viewing the poem as a fit of 'personal' and 'inner' verse, the product of variously a bad marriage, a breakdown, a botched homosexual love affair, but it stands as an address on public themes in largely public settings, one that laments the downfall of public order and shrieks of burning and toppling cities. In our own time, Robert Lowell's public/personal 'For the Union Dead' weaves a sequence of childhood memories into a fabric of public ills (racial hatreds, the bomb, the auto's conquest of the city). The death of public order proclaims itself in splendid public verse.

Thus, from the beginning of Lee's nine-poem sequence, when the speaker takes his position within Toronto's civic square and attempts to locate himself within that space, the reader knows that a vision of public affairs will follow. A gentler Juvenal has come to celebrate the city in the act of marking its fall.

Lee's first volume of poetry, *Kingdom of absence* (1967), attempted to sound the public note. In the quantum leap his writing made in the interval between it and *Civil elegies*, an introspective, anxiety-ridden set of personal lyrics masquerading as social statements assumed the power of the substantial intimations of public mortality that now appear.[42] The key term in his later sequence appears in the earlier *Kingdom* when the poet writes of attempting to colonize 'the void' ('Cities of the mind interred,' 11), but the idea remains undeveloped and mysterious until the later work.

We cannot consider the void before examining the world it describes. One of the sequence's epigraphs, on the hurt arising from acknowledging the impossibility of citizenship, comes from Grant's 'Canadian fate and imperialism.' It informs the audience that the nationalist interpretation of Canada's present economic and cultural state serves as an unquestioned 'given.' Canada has become a colony of the u.s., it shares complicity in that nation's unjust colonial war in Vietnam, its own culture has been swamped by America's, its leaders either approve of or are impotent in resisting this extinction of nationhood: these serve as premises.

What could in a less tough-minded writer become a series of self-pitying, self-hating, or self-exonerating complaints stands as an unblinking contemplation of the role our culture has played in its own destruction. If the ancestors, no more than 'Indian-swindlers, stewards of unclaimed earth and rootless,' showed in 1837 a collective cop-out on the part of peasants and patricians alike – 'the first / spontaneous mutual retreat in the history of warfare. / Canadians, in flight' – then what nobility remains?[43] None other than the ruthless domination necessary in the primal encounter with the land that 'broke the settlers ... till men who had worked their farms for a lifetime / could snap in a month from simple cessation of will' (3, 40). Out of this culture that viewed nature only in terms of domination and control comes the ironic fate of subjection to another's political and economic force. Nor can the subjection be dramatized in the hunger pangs of slavery, for the nation fattens on activities (such as investment) that require the support and benevolence of the ruling power. To realize this complexity and contradiction brings about an end to any sense of citizenship. It propels one across that terrifying gulf Grant wrote of that sets one apart from fellow countrymen. To experience this shocks one into a realization of the fall that has taken place:

Master and Lord, there was a
measure once.
There was a time when men could say
my life, my job, my home
and still feel clean.
The poets spoke of earth and heaven. There were no symbols. (2, 38)

However insubstantial the Eden invoked, the demands of mythology force
the speaker to name it, to give the process of degeneration a starting point in
contrast to the endless middle that drags on.

'Home' forms the sequence's antonym to 'void,' and the conclusion sounds
what seems to be a paradox when it counsels seeking a new home in that void.
A number of objects attempt to organize the poem's space in order to
transform it from void into home. The civic-square setting presents an open
space defined by the governmental structures of a lost citizenship. The Henry
Moore sculpture in the square in Toronto, like Wallace Stevens' jar in
Tennessee, radiates what ought to be organizational energies for the field.
Geoffrey Scott's *The architecture of humanism* recalls an historian's moving
account of the actual and symbolic weight of the obelisk set up before St
Peter's in order to define the centrality of the papal, new Roman imperial
ordering of the globe.[44] The poet here searches for a similar resonance in
Moore's 'Archer' (3, 39–40). Like Rilke's Apollonian torso, the sculpture
demands of its viewer some grander response to life, a response no longer
possible for everyday persons. 'But once at noon ... / the only resonance that
held was in the Archer' that 'was shaped by earlier space ... / flexed by blind
aeonic throes.' Beyond the sculpture's force-field, men in their daily lives
enter into void and themselves become part of it.

The civic square – and I paraphrase Lee's marginalia to an earlier draft of
this study – calls the citizens to a more resonant, resolute public experience.
They then return to their dwellings in a city deaf to that call: 'back to the
concrete debris, to parking-scars and the four-square tiers / of squat and
righteous lives' (1, 33). In time, the space will lose its charge, and stand as a
vacancy within the large orb of the American empire. In such a place, how lost
are even the words seeking to summon up our 'Master and Lord,' as the
second elegy points out. The fifth, like a later poem, 'The Death of Harold
Ladoo' (1976, reprinted with alterations in *The gods*), deals with a world that
has banished the gods only to have them return as demons. The demonic
ramps its way through a world in which playful children in the square remind
the viewer of napalmed children elsewhere.

After such knowledge, what forgiveness? Unlike Margaret Avison's splendid civic poem, 'To Professor X, Year Y' (1960), with its hints of apocalypse lurking behind quotidian urban unrest, no drama of destructive release lies in the wings of Lee's purgatorial pageant. It is not enough, we are told, 'to rail and flail at a dying civilisation,' nor can the mind offer its own refuge. Instead, that very will the settlers had to rely on – in this case, 'the long will to be in Canada' – must sustain us in our symbolic recrossing of the Atlantic and the new re-entry into Canada. The long haul is what concerns the poet (9, 56–7).

And yet the term 'void' keeps appearing, becoming no longer a vacuum but a state we must earn our right to exist in. The reader recalls the dark night of the Spanish mystics, the sense of deprivation which one earns through frugality and discipline, a space in which we ready ourselves for the still small voice that will sustain and illuminate us along our earthly path. Only by beginning from that felt void, as opposed to the one we ignore by our daily busyness, can we hope to make a home of here.

To paraphrase the remarks of the poet, the cycle of poems can be seen as a dialogue between political and religious concepts of void. Out of the latter, with its sense of a wilderness to be experienced before viewing Canaan, comes a sense of deprival in hope. The religious experience itself consists of an alteration between hope and its absence, at least as I myself know it. What the poems finally say is that this process of relinquishment, of stripping down, forces one to abandon both nationalist and 'voidish' comforts, and seek to make a home of wherever one stands, however impoverished the spot may be. Whatever remains, whatever of self remains, has been tested.

A glance at *Savage fields* (1977), Lee's critical volume, helps our understanding of the poems. Striving to locate a new common ground of literary experience, it conveys the same sense of spatiality that forms *Civil elegies'* viewpoint. In the third elegy, the space governed by the Archer coexists with the chaotic space of everyday life. Anyone strolling through the square lives within both spaces simultaneously. So man in *Savage fields* lives at once in a world of his own making, one of 'houses and laws and dictionaries' on an earth marked by non-man, by 'trees and mountains and animals.'[45] To move much too quickly through a gnomic and complex work, we may say that it teaches that a world-view segmenting man's experience into one kingdom or another creates disturbances in both. The literature that best handles the modern experience, the argument proceeds, conveys the extreme tensions inherent in such bifurcation through showing an increasing struggle between the two competing spaces. In an era when the subjection of earth to the

demands of world provokes from the former an increasingly unwilling response, the complex intersections between both induce a special agony.†
Savage fields, Lee's term for the complex reality we live in, finds an emblem in electromagnetism. Particles can exist simultaneously within two force fields – think here of the Archer, and everyday life – and behave according to the demands exerted by both fields, as the particles dance to the tune of both forces at the same time. Empire/Canada, banality/transcendence, impotence/mastery: artists like Tom Thomson and Saint-Denys-Garneau offer us examples of figures who – at some cost – made themselves at home in both worlds. But if the Quebec poet created resonant markers out of the emptiness sensed in himself and others, great art is not enough. Reconciliation stems from making a 'here' out of our own life and work (2, 40–1; 4, 45; 8, 52–3).

The term 'reconciliation' presents a distorted view of the sequence's conclusion, since courage and endurance to bear our divided lot form the final message. Because the poet does not try to tie up a series of conflicts within a conciliatory knot, the reader must rest content with the contemplative acceptance of division and renunciation as a way of coming to grips with our situation now.

Lee's pattern of human experience parallels Grant's: the fall, existence within a reality split off from a nobler world, the resolve to pursue whatever illuminations of the good exist in other places and persons. When Grant commends 'listening or watching or simply waiting for intimations of deprival which might lead us to see the beautiful as the image, in the world, of the good,' he seems not that far distant from *Civil elegies'* final prayer that earth, in its complexity addressed as both 'strangest' and 'nearest,' serve as home to us (9: 57).[46] The exile strives to locate adequate ground for being in the strange environment that forces mightier than he have thrust him into. In this dilemma, the Loyalist experience is reaffirmed.

To be cast out and not despair, to know that the time spent in struggle is not lost, to hope: these are states of feeling we associate with religious experience. In his linkage of secular struggle with religious resolve and hope, Lee reverses that reification of experience discussed in the last chapter. In viewing his own plight and ours in grander terms, he recalls that rendering of socio-political predicament into moral typology that has marked our culture from its very beginnings.

† Personification seems unavoidable here. Part of our difficulty in arranging these matters well stems from a vocabulary inadequate to express their complex, intertwined relationship. Can we even speak of earth, for example, without implicitly turning it into world?

V

The fences seen on the jacket drawing of Hood's *A new Athens* mark time
zones for Al Purdy's perspective on the transitory nature of all things. The
'ziggs of zagging snake fences / loyalist farmers measured long ago' form a
broken line connecting past and present corners of history.[47] Purdy's sense of
ancestry is wider than his use of UEL forbears in his work. He claims kinship
with Beothuck Indians ('Beothuck Indian Skeleton in Glass Case'), ancient
cavemen ('In the Foothills'), extinct Eskimo tribesmen ('Lament for the
Dorsets') and all sorts of figures – even to prehistoric creatures ('In the
Bearpaw Sea') – whose contribution either to the human project or to the
stream of life in general moves him to compassionate utterance. Yet this figure
who has created poetry that, as a critic observes, 'manages to be domestic and
historical at the same time,' employs the Loyalist fact extensively in his
lengthiest examination of his own line.[48] *In search of Owen Roblin* remains
something of a fabricated book, since it consists of a number of earlier and
superb poems strung together for broadcast purposes with filler verse of
inferior quality. Fortunately, Purdy discarded the gratuitous linkage when
placing the poems within his latest collected edition (*Being alive*).[49] Yet the
volume has the virtue of offering a continuous treatment of a landscape as it
exists in time. It represents the lengthiest attention he has bestowed on any
one scene, and that scene's meaning is closely knit with the poet's Loyalist
ancestry.

His meditation on Upper Canada / Ontario sprang from the most typical of
romantic roots: the contemplation of a ruin. In 1957–8, Purdy began poking
about an abandoned grist mill in Ameliasburgh, Ontario, the Loyalist-
founded village where he lives. He grew interested in the history of the ruin
and its details (24-inch-wide flooring, wooden cogs, hand-carved gears). The
year 1964 saw the first poem to well out of that interest.[50] The mill of Owen
Roblin, who once commanded the wealth and industry of the village and then
died at ninety-three to have it all pass with him, would naturally capture
Purdy's attention. As Eli Mandel has noted, he is a poet with 'a terrifying
sense of the elusiveness of experience ... the patterns that never succeeded.'[51]
This interest eventually produced a work affirming Purdy's ties with his
ancestry and their struggles. Earlier works – 'Wilderness Gothic,' 'My
Grandfather's Country,' and 'The Country North of Belleville,' for example
– strike another tone, giving us not only a sense of Purdy's ambiguity but a
realization of the ambiguities inherent in Loyalism itself. Briefly, Purdy's

poem about covenant contrasts with earlier treatments of a similar landscape that speak of Fall.

Purdy finishes his sequence of Roblin poems with a conclusion taken from one of the earlier works, 'Roblin's Mills (2),' as disintegration finds itself faced with determined affirmation of the dead:

> all things laid aside
>   discarded
>   forgotten
> but they had their being once
> and left a place to stand on[52]

This 'positive' version of Loyalism stresses covenantal transmission and endurance. The ancestors' accomplishments will continue and flourish if the heirs will but keep faith. In a world whose chronology has jumbled, the Loyalists remain an influence, however distant. They have as firm a right as anyone to lodge in the poet's mind:

> Time that tick-tocks always in my body
> its deadly rhythm is only a toy of the mind
> so that I leap back and forth
> from the American Revolution to my grandfather
> from Owen Roblin back to the Loyalists (52)

In fact, insofar as the rugged pioneering experience recalls the poet's own stressful life, the Loyalists remain with him as dour muses, tight-lipped inspirers of his own verse.

> I began to stop feeling sorry for myself
> taking strength from them
> not their coattails simply hanging on
> for a free ride that cost them nothing
> because there was no free ride for them
> they were born and loved and died
> and nothing came easy for them
> and dammit nothing is easy for me
> Anyhow I feel related to them
> by more than blood and just space they occupied

as if I too had hacked at monster trees
...
and felt what I couldn't say
except somehow they gave me the words (43)

These resolute, embittered and enduring figures thrust at the poet a demythologized, unheroic version of his own history that encloses him and his forbears in common bonds of humanity.

I tried to feel as they felt and think as they did
thrown out of their homes farther south
the new land bleak and forbidding
promising nothing but work and more work
some of the new settlers middleaged
others not more than boys
knowing how they were trapped
by the circumstance of loyalty
and trapped by their own stubbornness
even their weakness and pride
But not heroes
in any conventional sense
certainly not the brawny men I once imagined
striding through the forest that names their names
still impressed on faces of descendants
not heroes but people like all of us
all different and all human (42)

From this consideration of the facts of persistence and struggle the poet gains the sense of continuity and obligation closing the entire work.

The trouble with the Loyalists themselves in the Roblin sequence lies in their generalized evocation. Anonymity and the absence of heroic mythologizing is one thing, but thinness of detail is another. Thus, the only face to emerge from the crowd is that of a spunky woman nearly shot for declaring her loyalty to the king (35). Again, the point here is not to judge the poet by a very incidental work, but to use it to delineate his wrestlings with a sense of heritage. Thus one of Purdy's finest poems appears in his Loyalist sequence. The image of his grandfather appears central to his imagination. Left to itself, and placed within its final 'collected' context, the poem conveys no ancestor-worshipping reassurance, but the disquieting implications of extinction.

'Elegy for a Grandfather' appeared first in 1956 and, after extensive revision, again in 1968. It was lodged alongside a number of other formerly discrete pieces in the Roblin poems before coming to rest in *Being alive*.⁵³ The grandfather appears decidedly mythic. His death seems questionable ('Well, he died I guess. They say he did'), his skeleton gigantic ('His wide whalebone hips will make a prehistoric barrow / men of the future may find and perhaps not'). Death snatches extraordinary things, and he forms no exception to that, yet the grandfather in some way survives in that he is biologically and spiritually present in his descendant: 'and such a relayed picture perhaps / outlives any work of art, / survives among its alternatives' (54-5). That sort of consolation amid extinction occurs elsewhere in Purdy, in poems as various as 'Lament for the Dorsets' and 'Dark Landscape.'⁵⁴ Within the context of the Roblin poems, the 'Elegy' stands out as a fully realized instance of the vision of endurance that is the message in his treatment of the Loyalists.

A striking phrase in the 'Elegy' reminds the reader of an alternative to the mood of affirmation, when he reads that 'a sticky religious voice / folded [the grandfather's] century sideways to get it out of sight.' Eras can be wiped out, systems of thought bury all that has gone before. No thick dividing line can be drawn between the Roblin poems and such lyrics as 'My Grandfather's Country,' 'The Country North of Belleville,' and 'Wilderness Gothic,' though it is fair to say that if the Roblin sequence emphasizes survival and regeneration despite frustration and struggle, then the latter trio stresses the inertial and destructive aspects of experience. Purdy writes that humanity universally fears 'that when we die and our bones rot, our unimportant lives forgotten, even our descendants will harbour no trace in themselves of what we were. The ongoing wave of time will not carry us with it: we will be what we are in our most spiritually depressed moments – nothing.'⁵⁵ That fear thrusts itself into the forefront of these poems, with their brooding intimation that a sharp and discontinuous break has happened. Their inclusion in the Roblin sequence, with its preservationist message, dulls their bite a little. In both their original and final forms, they regain their keenness.

That sticky religious voice in the 'Elegy' wails its way toward silence in 'Wilderness Gothic,' which concludes with the prediction of a fall. Steeplejacks sheathe a church spire while the Gothic structure elides in the poet's mind with a picture of a self-assured rural culture of the sort that is caught in Grant Wood's popular American painting, *American Gothic*. The assurance, however, is breaking up, as ancestors peer out of family albums in bewilderment at what various omens portend, including the necessity to have the church repaired. Then the poet concludes that 'Perhaps [the workman] will fall.' The reader here has to avoid overblown allusions to the fall of man and to Ibsen's steeple-climber in *The master builder*, and yet insist that the poem presents a number of images of cultural dislocation and disintegration ('An age and a faith moving into transition, / the dinner cold and new-baked bread a failure'). Stillness marks the mood of the poem, which proceeds as a succession of still shots rather than as a continuous kinetic process. The religion-based culture of Owen Roblin on the verge of toppling, the speaker's detached observation of this moment: the poem's use of these motifs gives the reader a sense of distances unbridged, of modes of understanding we cannot guess our way back to.

The 'wave of time' Purdy spoke of in his account of the great fear has drowned 'The Country North of Belleville,' a 'country of our defeat':

> Old fences drift vaguely among the trees
>   a pile of moss-covered stones
> gathered for some ghost purpose
> has lost meaning under the meaningless sky
>   – they are like cities under water
> and the undulating green waves of time
>   are laid on them –

Even if that country, its poor farmlands reduced to drowned Atlantises, has not made its last stand as a human habitation ('sometime / we may go back there'), the distance, as in 'Wilderness Gothic,' between ourselves and home remains vast.

> But it's been a long time since
> and we must enquire the way
>   of strangers –

The voice that in the 'Elegy' folded the century sideways yielded to an image of immortality through progeny. That consolation halts at the barrier against reconciliation seen in 'The Country North of Belleville.'

'My Grandfather's Country,' 'where failed farms sink back into earth / the clearings join and fences no longer divide' reminds the reader of the land north of Belleville as well as all those other Purdy landscapes where time has weathered the landmarks we call our heritage. Behind all these stopped clocks lies the perpetual motion one of biology, the life force pushing all things along a wave of metamorphic continuation. Through that force, with its genetic codes that remember 'the protein formula / from the invincible mold / the chemicals that after solution select themselves,' we tumble onward in a promiscuous blending of forms:

> where the running animals gather their bodies together
> and pour themselves upward
> with the tips of falling leaves
> with mindless faith that presumes a future.

This universe of microcosm and macrocosm, where 'leaves fall in my grandfather's country / and mine too for that matter' at once contains and destroys the meaning of history. Things endure, if only through a process of relentless recycling. Yet, like a single note of currency left in a bank, individuality merges into the anonymity of greater combinations. No one can predict where any achievement or release of energy will eventually be put.

The securities of Roblin Lake need be no more enduring than the one-time boundaries so mashed together in time's mortar. When his work is viewed as a whole, Purdy's use of local habitation presents a picture at once affirmative and disturbing, with Loyalism both an enduring covenantal model of experience and another of the historical processes to be merged into the oblivion that overtakes all objects across the chasm of time. This forgetful-ness, we often experience as a fall.

VI

The writers in this chapter exemplify the extent to which a habit of mind based on a lengthy historical record persists in the literature of Ontario. Can the existence of this sensibility be shown without reducing a widespread human preoccupation to a single historical root? The enterprise repays the risk if it convinces the reader of the existence of a set of concerns tying together a number of diverse writers of the same time and place. Out of such an awareness can grow a sense of a culture's complexity and its dogged endurance. If the people who lived at once as Americans and monarchists, victims and founders, heroes and the dispossessed have left us with anything, surely it is a sense of those two abiding aspects of their experience.

Envoi

As I write this in 1980–1, the central failure of any Canadian nationalism – its inability to transcend regionalism – impresses itself upon me. If this is a price we pay for a federal rather than a unitary state, then so be it. Yet I cannot help wondering if that is an inescapable price.

I came to that sense of failure through writing this study. I began it with the expectation that I was after a particular aspect of the English Canadian mind. The thread I pursued among the writers of my own (adopted) region would also, I assumed, show itself elsewhere. I planned, in short, another CanLit theme book. Eventually I realized that my limits lay between Lake Huron and the Ottawa River. Even the Loyalist Maritime provinces proved off limits, because the military component had given Upper Canadian Loyalism a combative and triumphal flavour I detected nowhere else.

Take the most visible political questions of the last decade – Quebec, energy, the constitution – they all reduce themselves finally to questions of regionalism. One cannot quarrel with facts, but only observe their implications. Regionalism's chief weakness is that it does render our country all the more vulnerable to the domination of the United States. Yet a Canadian nationalism whose only widely accepted doctrine is that of anti-Americanism cannot generate the energies necessary to retain this country's independence.

Does this mean then that our future lies in serving as quasi-autonomous marches for the American heartland? Perhaps; yet I was struck while pursuing this study by the fact that a region found sufficient relevance in its own beginnings to create from that a vision of nationhood.† Not only did

† Its gains and losses are clearly set out in Allan Smith, 'Old Ontario and the emergence of a national frame of mind,' in F.H. Armstrong, H.A. Stevenson, and J.D. Wilson, eds., *Aspects of nineteenth-century Ontario* (Toronto: University of Toronto Press 1974), 194–217.

Loyalism help produce that vision, but it gave us a kind of cultural fall-out that persists still. A habit of mind that emphasizes loss and the prospect of loss, the fall of traditions of civility, proclaims itself in our literature over the decades and down to the present.

To deal with the manifestations of a regional mind is a tricky business. It is to stand at the corner where Mythology runs into Politics, and dash into the middle of the intersection in the hope that one can slow the traffic long enough to get a glimpse of its flow. Thus, even in a region with as historic, embattled, and articulated a consciousness as the American South, critics and probers can debate to the world's end the connections between its own racial system and those of other societies. And here is a scholarly field well harvested over the centuries. How much more tentative and inexact must be my own efforts!

Despite all this, I have attempted to trace in hops and jumps a vital tradition in the literature of Upper Canada / Ontario. And what, finally, is the message of that tradition? It is a simple one: Canada makes no sense except as part of a larger political, social, and cultural entity. To some, this offers no more than yet another reiteration of a colonial mentality. And yet, what grounds are there to support a concept of cultural autarky for a nation not created by revolution and which came into being during the modern age as a product of imperial drives? Does this then mean that we are forever fated to exist within *some* empire or other, since empires provide the material base that grants the surest hope for the continuation of a tradition? Yes, if empires continue to provide that material base. But will the present age of empire last forever? Can the present groupings of nations persist indefinitely? Can hope and passion not sustain us? And with that question, I must pass into the realm of theology, and state without argument my belief that nothing is ever lost. This is no more than an act of faith. Yet it is what sustains me.

The ampler Canada that Loyalism and its successors envisaged stays with us now largely in the cries of anguished renunciation that make so moving Lee's *Civil elegies.* That anguish – far from ignoble or self-pitying – came out of a sense of one-time rootedness. The anguish of Lee and other writers is not monolithic. The pain of loss is not Loyalism's alone. But whatever ideal of decency in the affairs of men belonged to that tradition was ours. Not perfect, not convincing to everyone, but ours: the noblest product Ontario had to offer to the rest of Canada. Yet that vision, sectionalized, misappropriated, its rhetoric employed to justify the smashing of the alternative Canada that had sprung from the Métis experience, still came from our own cultural and historical experience. It could have been refined rather than discarded.

This work has made a few wild stabs at pinpointing one of the cultural forces that gave Ontario its sense of place. That exploration of defeat and displacement reveals that many of our roots were once here, and deeply felt. Even to behold that with the pain of loss has been for me, a born and bred outsider, an act of hope.

Notes

INTRODUCTION

1 The desire for an explicit and dramatic beginning has made this landing the curtain-raiser for the Loyalist fact in Ontario, though in fact refugees had been trickling into the fortified Niagara region while the Revolutionary war was still in progress.

2 Thomas Raddall's novel *His majesty's Yankees* (1942) offers a convincing and entertaining portrait of this sort of reluctant allegiance as it took place in Nova Scotia.

3 Late Loyalist was the name given the land-hungry Americans who moved to Upper Canada in the years before 1812 and took an oath of allegiance to the crown.

4 The material from the *Canadian Magazine* remains most accessible in J.J. Talman, ed., *Loyalist narratives from Upper Canada* (Toronto: Champlain Society 1946), 149–266. Quotations are taken from this text.

5 See Allan Smith, 'Old Ontario and the emergence of a national frame of mind,' in F.H. Armstrong, H.A. Stevenson, and J.D. Wilson, eds., *Aspects of nineteenth-century Ontario* (Toronto: University of Toronto Press 1974), 194–217.

6 Letter of the Reverend John Stuart, 26 Nov. 1798. Quoted in Catherine S. Crary, ed., *The price of loyalty: Tory writings from the Revolutionary era* (New York: McGraw Hill 1973), 452. One of the most influential of early Upper Canadian Loyalists, John Stuart played the role of 'spiritual father' to the Reverend John Strachan. See G.A. Rawlyk, 'The Reverend John Stuart: Mohawk missionary and reluctant Loyalist,' in Esmond Wright, ed., *Red, white, and true blue: the Loyalists in the Revolution* (New York: AMS 1976), 55–71.

7 Another dweller in the Upper Canadian wilderness, Susanna Moodie, took the

same view. Despite various parallels between her observations and those of the writers treated here, I have not included her writings on account of my conviction that her total work fails to come close enough to the preoccupations studied. While her reactions to 1837 stress the theme of her and her job-seeking husband's loyalty, they proceed from an accepted rather than an examined rhetoric. My contention is that such rhetoric remains much more deliberately employed by the writers in this essay.

CHAPTER ONE

1 George M. Wrong, *Canada and the American Revolution* (Toronto: Macmillan 1935), 283ff.
2 J.B. Brebner, *The neutral Yankees of Nova Scotia* ... (Toronto: McClelland and Stewart [1969]), 275; Gordon Stewart and George Rawlyk, *A people highly favoured of God* (Toronto: Macmillan 1972), 73.
3 See Mary Beth Norton, *The British-Americans* (Boston: Little, Brown 1972), passim.
4 'The reception of the American Loyalists by Great Britain in the year 1783' (1788) appears in finished form only as an inset in West's *Portrait of John Eardley-Wilmot, esq., 1812*. An engraving of the never-finished *grande machine* may be found as the frontispiece to Hugh E. Egerton, ed., *Royal Commission on the losses and services of the American Loyalists, 1783–5* (Oxford: University Press 1951). See also Mary Beth Norton, 'Eardley-Wilmot, Britannia, and the Loyalists: a painting by Benjamin West,' *Perspectives in American History* VI (1972): 119–31.
5 Piers Mackesy, *The war for America, 1755–1783* (London: Longmans 1964), 337.
6 ' "Ah." So I am under fire at last!" he said to himself. "I have seen shots fired!" he repeated with a sense of satisfaction. "Now I am a real soldier." At that moment, the escort began to go hell for leather, and our hero realized that it was shot from the guns that was making the earth fly up all around him. He looked vainly in the direction from which the balls were coming, he saw the white smoke of the battery at an enormous distance, and, in the thick of the steady and continuous rumble produced by the artillery fire, he seemed to hear shots discharged much closer at hand; he could not understand in the least what was happening.' Stendhal, *The Charterhouse of Parma*, trans. C.K. Scott Moncrieff (1839; New York: Liverwright 1924), I: 54.
7 Robert C. Calhoon, *The Loyalists in Revolutionary America, 1760–1781* (New York: Harcourt, Brace, Jovanovich 1973), 218; Hiller B. Zobel, *The Boston massacre* (New York: W.W. Norton 1970), passim.

8 Wallace Brown, *The king's friends* (Providence: Brown University Press 1965), 37–8.
9 See Wallace Brown, *The good Americans* (New York: William Morrow 1969), 82–125; W.H. Nelson, *The American Tory* (Oxford: Clarendon Press 1961), 18–20.
10 A wealth of information and informed speculation exists concerning the sort of regions strong in Tories (occupied towns and 'regions already in decline, or not yet risen to importance' [Nelson, *American Tory*, 87]), and the kinds of occupations and social groupings likely to engender them (Brown, *King's friends*, 282), but no consensus of historians has come up with 'the typical Tory' or even a social group (beyond Quakers and Highlanders) that could be viewed as generally Tory in allegiance. Not even office-holding offers a certain indication of Loyalist conviction (Anne Alden Allan, 'Patriots and Loyalists: the choice of political allegiances by the members of Maryland's proprietary elite,' *Journal of Southern History* 38 [1972]: 283–92). The matter is quickly summed up by Kenneth D. McRae in 'The structure of Canadian history,' in Louis Hartz, ed., *The founding of new societies* (New York: Harcourt, Brace and World 1964), 237: 'There is no simple criterion to explain the incidence of Loyalism during the Revolution. American society split vertically almost from top to bottom. Factors of geography, military campaigning, local politics and private vendettas all added their weight to political and economic considerations. Many, as the Loyalist claims amply prove, changed allegiance during the war, and families were often split within themselves. All of which demonstrates that we are not dealing here with a simple social revolution of class against class.'
11 Observe, for example, the pre-Revolutionary career and writings of Joseph Galloway in Calhoon, *Loyalists*, 85–90, and Nelson, *American Tory*, 47–63.
12 See Bernard Bailyn, *Ideological origins of the American Revolution* (Harvard: Belknap Press 1967), passim.
13 Bernard Bailyn, *The ordeal of Thomas Hutchinson* (Cambridge: Belknap Press 1974), 221–59.
14 See, for example, North Callahan, *Royal raiders* (Indianapolis: Bobbs-Merrill 1963), 105–6.
15 Paul H. Smith, 'The American Loyalists: notes of their organization and numerical strength, *William and Mary Quarterly* ser. 3, 25 (1968): 259–77.
16 See the accounts collected in Catherine S. Crary, *The price of Loyalty: Tory writings from the Revolutionary era* (New York: McGraw Hill 1973), 171–85. An interesting speculation on the psychological effects on the British high command of this sort of warfare may be found in John Shy, 'Armed Loyalism: the case of the lower Hudson valley,' in his *A people numerous and armed* (New York: Oxford University Press 1976), 181–92.

17 Mackesy, *War for America*, 251–6.
18 D.C. Scott, *John Graves Simcoe* (Toronto: Morang 1905), 37.
19 Paul H. Smith, *Loyalists and redcoats* (Chapel Hill: University of North Carolina Press 1964), 141.
20 The briefest and best survey of American Loyalist historiography is in Wallace Brown, 'Loyalist historiography,' *Acadiensis* IV (autumn 1974): 133–8.
21 Brown, *The good Americans*, 227, 173.
22 The Niagara region had been a British frontier outpost since 1759, and by 1780 refugee veterans of Butler's Rangers had begun to settle there. However, the planting of the Loyalists at that place did not take place with the forethought of the settlements along the Bay of Quinte.
23 J.J. Talman, 'The United Empire Loyalists,' in *Profiles of a province* (Toronto: Ontario Historical Society 1967), 4–5.
24 George Rawlyk, 'Canada and the American Revolution,' *Queen's Quarterly* 83 (autumn 1976): 380.
25 See E.A. Cruikshank, 'A study of disaffection in Upper Canada in 1812–1815' and 'The County of Norfolk in the war of 1812,' and W.R. Riddell, 'The Ancaster "Bloody Assize" of 1814,' in Morris Zaslow, ed., *The defended border* (Toronto: Macmillan 1964), 205–23, 224–40, 241–50.
26 A 'Come-all-you' folk-ballad commemorating Brock's victory at Detroit was still being sung in Canadian lumber camps more than one hundred years later (Irwin Silber, ed., *Songs of independence* [Harrisburg, Pa.: Stackpole Books 1973], 194–5).
27 See C.P. Stacey, 'The war of 1812 in Canadian history,' in Zaslow, ed., *Defended border*, 331–7, and George F.G. Stanley, 'The constitution of the Canadian militia during the war,' in Philip P. Mason, ed., *After Tippecanoe* (Toronto: Ryerson 1963), 28–48.
28 'The U.E. Loyalists have been as a barrier of rock, against which the waves of Republicanism have dashed in vain.' William Canniff, *The settlement of Upper Canada* (1869; new ed., Belleville: Mika 1971), 634. The first study of the Loyalist impact on Upper Canada, Canniff's work is a huge, disorganized volume that remains valuable for its wealth of detail not only about political history but for its accounts of ecclesiastical politics and agricultural practices. Though the author was a member of Canada First and a key organizer of the centennial celebrations of the Loyalist landings (see Donald Swainson's introduction to the new edition), and while he delivers|a special encomium on the UEL (616–24), the myths of Loyalism are not as fully or forcefully articulated by Canniff as by others. Thus Canniff's work remains of lesser interest to this study.
29 W.S. Wallace, *The United Empire Loyalists* (Toronto: Glasgow, Brooke 1914), 111.

30 A case in point is the legal / illegal harassment, imprisonment, and expulsion of
Robert Gourlay in 1818–19: D.B. Read, *The Canadian rebellion of 1837*
(Toronto: C. Blackett Robinson 1896), 105–12.

31 *The centennial of the settlement of Upper Canada by the United Empire
Loyalists, 1784–1884* (Toronto: Rose Publishing Co. 1885), 9–124. A masterly
treatment of Loyalism's role as a political mythology at this time is Carl
Berger, *The sense of power* (Toronto: University of Toronto Press 1970), 78–108.

32 Though some Loyalists proved disloyal in 1812 (Talman, 'United Empire Loyalists,' 5), the 1812 myth would survive intact in popular history as late as 1932,
when A.G. Bradley's *The United Empire Loyalists* (London: Thornton Butter-
worth) appeared. One-third of the text is devoted to 1812–15.

33 Clara Thomas, *Ryerson of Upper Canada* (Toronto: Ryerson 1969), 3, 133.

34 Quotation from J.M. Bumstead, 'William Smith, Jr., and *The history of
Canada*' in Lawrence H. Leder, ed., *The colonial legacy; vol. I: The Loyalist
historians* (New York: Harper & Row 1971), 204.

35 Marion MacRae and Anthony Adamson, *Hallowed walls* (Toronto: Clarke,
Irwin 1975), 16–47. For the 'Americanism' of rank and file Nova Scotian Loyal-
ists, see Neil MacKinnon, 'Nova Scotia Loyalists, 1783–85,' *Histoire sociale /
Social History* no. 4 (Nov. 1969): 47–8.

36 Egerton Ryerson, *The Loyalists of America and their times: from 1620 to 1816*
(2nd ed., Toronto: Wm. Briggs 1880), I: 481. For Tory conspiracy theories, see
Calhoon, *Loyalists*, 234–43, 263; G.N.D. Evans, ed., *Allegiance in America:
the case of the Loyalists* (Reading, Mass.: Addison Wesley 1969), 64–5; Norton,
British-Americans, 130–46; John A. Schultz, 'Joseph Galloway's *Historical
and political reflections*,' in Leder, ed., *Colonial legacy*, I: 83–7. For Whig conspiracy theories, see Bernard Bailyn, *The origins of American politics* (New
York: Knopf 1968), 11–13, and also his 'General introduction' to *Pamphlets of
the American Revolution* (Cambridge: Harvard University Press 1965), I:
60–89.

37 Lorenzo M. Sabine, *Biographical sketches of Loyalists of the American
Revolution* (1847; Boston: 1864).

38 Compact treatments of the political attitudes associated with Loyalism can be
found in Murray W. Barkley, 'The Loyalist tradition in New Brunswick,'
Acadiensis IV (spring 1975): 3–45, and in Jo-Ann Fellows, 'The Loyalist myth in
Canada,' Canadian Historical Association, *Historical papers, 1971*, 94–111.
Barkley's list of political values, except for the absence of the military compo-
nent, applies to Upper Canada as well as to the Maritimes.

CHAPTER TWO

1 Biographical information: Lorne Pierce, *William Kirby, the portrait of a Tory
Loyalist* (Toronto: Macmillan 1929), 1–35.

2 Pierce, *Kirby*, 34.

3 His wife's father had paid Kirby's way out of debtors' prison, where an absconding partner in his tannery had landed him. The extent of his personal cultivation can be gauged by his mealtime draughts of literature: French at breakfast, English at dinner, German at supper (*ibid.*, 54–6, 84).

4 Letter of 12 Mar. 1891 in Pierce, *Kirby*, 337.

5 This translation of a political / historical situation into a kind of personal theatre happens even in Kirby's biography, where the author accepts without comment the inclusive nature of Loyalism as defined by Kirby. Pierce adopts a precious literary style ('Merry he was rarely,' 245) and extends Loyalism's domain even to the erotic ('the fastidious ears of the Loyalist belles, those shell-like ears hidden in curls and dripping with ornaments,' 48).

6 For a discussion of Canada First and Loyalism, see Carl Berger, *The sense of power* (Toronto: University of Toronto Press 1970), 49–108; for the New Imperialism, see R.C. Brown and R. Cook. *Canada, 1896–1921: a nation transformed* (Toronto: McClelland and Stewart 1974), 26–48.

7 W.R. Riddell, *William Kirby* (Toronto: Ryerson 1925), 157.

8 Some sense of Kirby's adherence to older forms of literary expression, despite an awareness of what was current, arises from reflecting that he read with interest *The brothers Karamazov* before it had been translated into English (Pierce, *Kirby*, 247) and yet continued to write narrative poems in blank verse. Though an exact date for his reading of the novel is not given, the work first appeared in Russian in 1880. No English translation appeared until 1912, but Kirby could have read the French translation of 1888. The context in which the statement of his having read the novel appears would seem to place it before the publication of his *Canadian idylls* (Welland, Ont. 1894).

9 Kirby, *Canadian idylls*, 64–80, esp. 71ff.

10 Kirby, *Annals of Niagara* (Welland, Ont. 1896), 85; *The U.E., a tale of Upper Canada* (1859; reprint ed., Toronto: University of Toronto Press 1973), canto 4, stanza 21.

11 Kirby's Loyalist centennial speech in 1884, with its Virgilian evocation of Loyalists bearing their 'penates and household gods' out of the U.S., can be found in his *Canadian idylls*, 168. The importance of the oration in setting forth the figures of the Loyalist myth can be gauged by the fact of its inclusion in Colonel Denison's article on 'The United Empire Loyalists' in J. Castell Hopkins, ed., *Canada: an encyclopedia of the country* I (Toronto 1898), 107.

12 See Northrop Frye, 'Conclusion,' in Carl F. Klinck, ed., *Literary history of Canada* (Toronto: University of Toronto Press 1965), 824.

13 See the following narratives in Talman, 'United Empire Loyalists': Thomas Gummersall Anderson 2–3, Catharine White 358–9, Susan Burnham Greeley 107, and James Dittrick 68–9.

14 See Riddell, *Kirby*, 64 n4, and Kirby, *Canadian idylls*, 24. An anecdote from 'Tiger' Dunlop's 1812 memoirs of his service on the Niagara front presents the family-feud nature of this warfare. A UEL militiaman begins to rifle the body of an enemy soldier he has just shot. 'On examining [the victim's] features he discovered that it was his own brother … He took possession of his valuables, consisting of an old silver watch and a clasp knife, his rifle and appointments, coolly remarking that it "served him right for fighting for the rebels, when all the rest of his family fought for King George"' (William Dunlop, *Tiger Dunlop's Upper Canada* [1847; Toronto: New Canadian Library 1967], 44–5).

15 For this theme in Mrs Moodie, see J.W. Foster, 'The poetry of Margaret Atwood,' *Canadian Literature* no. 74 (autumn 1977): 5–20.

16 Kirby, *Annals of Niagara*, 138–58, 179–207.

17 For Le Moine's essay, see *Maple leaves: Canadian history – literature – sports*, new ser. (Quebec: Augustin Coté 1873), 84–97. A number of other essays by Le Moine served as sources for Kirby and are mentioned in Pierce, *Kirby*, 236–8. As Pierce notes, Le Moine also wrote a piece on the adventures of Major Robert Stobo (55–63), which in turn inspired that other grand swashbuckling treatment of Old Quebec, Sir Gilbert Parker's *The seats of the mighty* (1896).

18 Elizabeth Waterston, *Survey: a short history of Canadian literature* (Toronto: Methuen 1973), 39.

19 William Kirby, *The golden dog (Le chien d'or), a romance of old Quebec* (Toronto: Musson [1925]), 1. This edition (illustrated by C.W. Jefferys) appears to be more widely available through libraries and used-bookshops than the 1969 New Canadian Library edition, and all subsequent references in the body of the text are to it. Since, however, all editions subsequent to the first were abridged by the author, some of the material in this chapter comes from that initial text: *Le chien d'or, the golden dog, a legend of Quebec* (New York and Montreal: Lovell, Adam, Wesson 1877). References to the 1925 edition are given in the text; references to the original edition appear in the notes.

20 Kirby, *Le chien d'or*, chap. XXIX, 410–15. On the speculative mythographers and their attempts through an unscientific comparative religion and philology to locate a common origin for the races of man, see E.B. Hungerford, *The shores of darkness* (New York: Columbia University Press 1941), and Ruthven Todd, 'William Blake and the eighteenth century mythologists,' in his *Tracks in the snow* (London: Grey Walls Press 1946), 29–60. North America as Atlantis occurs also in Kirby's 'Pontiac,' *Canadian idylls*, 69, where the Indian languages are given an Atlantean source. The degree to which Kirby actually believed this cannot be determined, but the sort of provincial intelligence that could both read 'Karamazov' and write pastoral idylls in blank verse would not appear incapable of discovering Atlantis close to home.

21 Riel, who if mad was but a little madder than any nationalist visionary,

carried the myth a stage westward and set up the 'true' papacy in the diocese of Montreal and its prophetic frontier among the Exovedate at Batoche.

22 Kirby, *Le chien d'or*, VI, 51.

23 Ibid., VII, 53; IV, 30.

24 Ibid., XXI, 217; XXVI, 267–8.

25 Carl F. Klinck, 'Literary activity in Canada, east and west, 1841–1880,' in Klinck, ed., *Literary history of Canada: Canadian literature in English* (2nd ed., 3 vols., Toronto: Univesity of Toronto Press 1976), I: 173.

CHAPTER THREE

1 It was typical of Richardson to publish a pamphlet, *The guards in Canada*, refuting the allegations that he was a card-sharp and thus ensure that they received even wider circulation.

2 For biographical information, see A.C. Casselman's 'Biography of Major John Richardson' in *Richardson's war of 1812* (1842; reprint ed., Toronto: Coles 1974); W. Renwick Riddell, *John Richardson* (Toronto: Ryerson 1923); David Beasley, *The Canadian Don Quixote: the life and works of Major John Richardson, Canada's first novelist* (Erin, Ont.: Porcupine's Quill 1977).

3 The Thackerayean (*Pendennis*), Grub Street nature of his final days is captured in a contemporary obituary notice: *The Pick* 1 (22 May 1852), quoted in Carl Ballstadt, ed., *Major John Richardson, a selection of reviews and criticism* (Montreal: L.M. Lande Foundation 1972), 53.

4 John Moss, *Patterns of isolation in English Canadian fiction* (Toronto: McClelland and Stewart 1974), 42.

5 'Here reposes / Maria Caroline / the Generous-Hearted / High-Souled / Talented and Deeply-Lamented Wife of Major Richardson / Knight of the Military Order of Saint Ferdinand / First Class / and Superintendant of Police on the Welland Canal during the Administration of Lord Metcalfe. This Matchless Wife and This [illegible] Exceeding Grief of Her Faithfully Attached Husband after a few days' illness at St. Catherine's on the 16 August, 1845, at the age of 37 years.' Casselman, 'Biography of Major John Richardson,' xxxviii.

6 David Beasley, 'Tempestuous major: the Canadian Don Quixote,' *Bulletin of the New York Public Library* 74 (Jan. 1970): 3; Desmond Pacey, 'A colonial romantic, Major John Richardson, soldier and novelist,' *Canadian Literature* no. 2 (autumn 1959): 21.

7 See chap. 1 notes 16 and 25; also, Kirby, *Annals of Niagara* (Welland, Ont. 1896), 188–9.

8 Sandra Djwa, in 'Letters in Canada, 1976,' *University of Toronto Quarterly*

XLVI (1977): 473–4. See also L.R. Early, 'Myth and prejudice in Kirby, Richardson, and Parker,' *Canadian Literature* no. 81 (summer 1979): 25–8.

9 Pacey, 'Colonial romantic,' 29.

10 R. Jones, 'Wacousta; or, the curse,' *Black Moss* ser. 2, no. 1 (spring 1976): 41–74. James Reaney's 1978 production of his own *Wacousta* (Toronto: Press Porcépic 1979) follows the novel's grim destructive path, with the addition of a major theme concerning the extinction of Indian culture. The use of toy cars, however, to depict what the course of history would later make the most prominent aspect of the site of Fort Detroit, indicates the drama's uneasy occupancy of a space somewhere between melodrama and farce.

11 To summarize the plot would delay (and perhaps confuse) the reader more than is necessary. Therefore a very simplified version of the story follows: Colonel De Haldimar and Reginald Morton, while subalterns in the British army, were rivals for the hand of sheltered Highland girl, Clara Beverley. De Haldimar won her through a trick, framing Morton on a charge that got him court-martialled and dismissed. Morton joined the French army and nearly killed one of De Haldimar's sons on the Plains of Abraham. By 1763, the time of Pontiac's conspiracy, Morton has become the renegade Wacousta, bloodthirstiest of Pontiac's advisors. The plot of the novel, set in the fort at Detroit at the time of the troubles, concerns itself with a bizarre series of events. Wacousta vengefully helps destroy most of De Halidmar's children before he is finally eliminated, leaving all but one child dead at the conclusion. Richardson, *Wacousta; or, the prophecy* (1832; Toronto: McClelland and Stewart 1923). All editions of *Wacousta*, except for the very first (London: T. Cadell 1832), have been abridged, though none to the extent of the 1967 New Canadian Library edition. The text used here is a representative, widely available example of the *Wacousta* that the vast majority of readers have encountered over the past century and a half. See Douglas Cronk, 'Bibliography,' in James Reaney, *Wacousta*, 161–3.

12 John Moss, *Patterns of isolation*, passim; *Sex and violence in the Canadian novel* (Toronto: McClelland and Stewart 1977), 84–90.

13 This favourite device of Richardson's is repeated in *The Canadian brothers*, where the villain, Desborough (Wacousta's son; they share superhuman strengths and *heldentenor* voices), appears in black-face. Westbrook, villain in a novel of that title, wears a mask during an attempted rape. See also Robert A. Lecker, 'Patterns of deception in *Wacousta*,' *Journal of Canadian Fiction* no. 19 (1977): 77–85.

14 This degeneration extends even to Westbrook's imitation of Milton's Satan when he peeks at the lovemaking of a young couple.

15 Margot Northey, *The haunted wilderness* (Toronto: University of Toronto Press 1976), 24–5.

16 Some of the complexities can be caught in a name. Frank Halloway is both frank in admitting the dereliction of duty for which the colonel has him shot, and hollow because he bears a false identity and thus is not free to explain the exonerating circumstances.

17 John Richardson, *The Canadian brothers; or, the prophecy fulfilled: a tale of the late American war* (1840; Toronto: University of Toronto Press 1976), 1: 207–20.

18 I cannot agree with Robin Mathews' argument that a plausible, humane alternative to the complementary horrors of both garrison and wilderness exists in the small French Canadian settlement that Richardson locates near the fort. Richardson simply fails to provide sufficient importance – whether narrative or symbolic – to that hamlet to give it the kind of weight Mathews discerns. It would be comforting if it did show the reader 'a social order which prizes land, wealth and people, but employs them creatively for everyone's freedom and benefit,' but we do not see the village often or fully enough to make that symbolic value, assuming it to exist, at all clear. Even the brightest stars cannot guide us on a cloudy night. See 'John Richardson: the Wacousta factor,' in Mathews, *Canadian Literature: surrender or revolution*, ed. Gail Dexter (Toronto: Steel Rail 1978), 17.

19 John Richardson, *Ecarté; or, the salons of Paris* (London: Henry Colburn 1829), 1: 63.

20 Richardson, *Wascousta*, 17; *Hardscrabble, a tale of Chicago*, published in five instalments in *Sartain's Union Magazine* VI (Jan.-June 1850), 393.

21 John Richardson, *Westbrook the outlaw* (1851; Montreal: Grant Woolner Books 1973), 1.

22 *Richardson's war of 1812*, 134, 158.

23 For a discussion of the officer-artists, see J. Russell Harper, *Painting in Canada* (Toronto: University of Toronto Press 1966), 41–55.

24 John Richardson, *Tecumseh and Richardson: the story of a trip to Walpole Island and Port Sarnia* (Toronto: Ontario Book Co. 1924), 65, 71. See also Richardson, *The Canadian brothers*, 1: 9. A fuller discussion of Richardson's Indian portraits occurs in Leslie Monkman, 'Richardson's Indians,' *Canadian Literature* no. 81 (summer 1979): 86–94.

25 John Richardson, *The monk knight of St. John* (New York: [Dewitt and Davenport 1850]), esp. 14–16, 27, and 145–55.

26 This commonplace of romantic observation constitutes a frequent motif throughout Richardson's fiction. See, for example, *Ecarté*, 1: 243; *Wacousta*, 172, 267; *Wau-nan-gee; or, the massacre at Chicago* (New York: H. Long & Brother 1852), 79.

27 John Richardson, *Eight years in Canada* (Montreal: H.H. Cunningham 1847), 117; *Westbrook*, 47.

28 One, the other, or both occur in every fictional work of Richardson's, with the exception of *Hardscrabble*. Both his poetic and historical accounts of Tecumseh's death make much of American attempts to flay the great chief's corpse.

29 The Crusades took place during a time when the 'cold and soul-annihilating conventionalisms of modern life were unknown,' and 'selfishness had not attained that refinement which progressive civilization has nurtured' (*The monk knight*, 8). In such an atmosphere, where a celibate touching a woman's breasts produces a 'triumph of nature over art – of truth over falsehood – of a hallowed and divine sentiment, over the cold and abstract conventionalisms of a world which, child-like, forges its own chains, fetters its own limbs, and glories in the display of its own bondage' (21), sex becomes 'the most exquisite proof of the boundless love of the Great God of the Universe' (40). The author also links sexual repression with the acquisitive, materialist nature of the New World, noting that 'we live a century too soon,' since a better age must be at hand (80).

CHAPTER FOUR

1 Glen Tucker, *Tecumseh; vision of glory* (Indianapolis: Bobbs-Merrill 1956), 325.

2 Allan W. Eckert, *Tecumseh! a play* (Boston: Little, Brown 1974), 169.

3 William Henry Harrison to War Department, 6 Aug. 1811, quoted in Carl F. Klinck, ed., *Tecumseh: fact and fiction in early records; a book of primary source materials* (Englewood Cliffs, NJ: Prentice-Hall 1961), 89. For an opponent's eyewitness appreciation, see 95–6.

4 Tecumseh's career attracted a number of biographers both in this century and the last. According to a recent authority, 'most 20th century writing on the brothers has been as bad as, if not worse than, that which was produced in the century before' (H.C.W. Goltz, Jr, 'Tecumseh, the Prophet and the rise of the Northwest Indian Confederation' [unpublished dissertation, University of Western Ontario 1973] 11). This he attributes to present-day writers' uncritical attitudes towards sources. According to Goltz, the earliest biography, Benjamin Drake's *The life of Tecumseh, and of his brother the Prophet* (1841; Cincinnati: E. Morgan 1850), is still the most reliable.

Tucker's *Tecumseh*, for all its inclusion of apocryphal material, remains the most readable of the various treatments and contains an ample bibliography. Klinck's anthology presents a useful range of contemporary opinion. 'Heroic' accounts of the Shawnee chief occur in Norman S. Gurd, *The story of Tecumseh* (Toronto: Wm. Briggs 1912), and Ethel T. Raymond, *Tecumseh* (Toronto: Glasgow Brook 1915). Gurd's work appeared as the second of a Canadian Heroes series whose first volume dealt with Brock.

5 Indians fleeing from defeat at the hands of the Americans after the battle of

Fallen Timbers in August 1794 found the gates at the British outpost of Fort Miami closed against them.

6 'A careful review piles up the evidence that the incitement to war did not come from the British to the Indians but from the Indians to the British': Tucker, *Tecumseh*, 180. Mair's drama, in act 3, scene 7, follows this view.

7 Quoted in George F.G. Stanley, 'The Indians in the war of 1812,' *Canadian Historical Review* XXXI (1950): 164.

8 See C.W. Jefferys, *Picture gallery of Canadian history*, vol. 2 (Toronto: Ryerson 1945), 155.

9 An account of this offensive defence by which Upper Canada was rallied – it has the advantage of being a first-hand narrative – remains Major Richardson's *War of 1812*.

10 Richardson, *War of 1812*, 154–5, 204–7, 212–3; *The Canadian brothers*, I, 9–12, 27, 142, 173; II 185–91. For those finding Richardson too biased an observer, Klinck's anthology contains a number of laudatory references to Tecumseh from friend and foe alike.

11 Major Richardson claimed that Tecumseh's body was mutilated for souvenirs, but it is far likelier that Tecumseh's remains were conveyed to an unknown grave before any indignities could be perpetrated upon it. See Klinck, ed., *Tecumseh*, 200–19. 'We have at least five Indian accounts of the death of Tecumseh. None of them agree' (Goltz, 'Tecumseh,' 5).

12 [John Richardson], *Tecumseh; or, the warrior of the west: a poem in four cantos, with notes* (London: R. Glynn 1828), v.

13 Charles Mair, *Tecumseh: a drama*, in *Dreamland and other poems and Tecumseh: a drama* (1886; reprint ed., intro. by Norman Shrive, Toronto: University of Toronto Press 1974).

14 Sarah Anne Curzon, *Laura Secord, the heroine of 1812, a drama; and other poems* (Toronto: C. Blackett Robinson 1887). Request to Mair: Norman Shrive, *Charles Mair: literary nationalist* (Toronto: University of Toronto Press 1965), 215. Mair would later glorify Laura Secord when in 1901 he 'Canadianized' his poem 'summer' and included her in this dream of fair women. He also in 1888 perpetrated a 'Ballad for Brave Women' that recites her story in a 'Twas the night before Christmas' metrical scheme.

15 Curzon, *Laura Secord*, iii. On Rebecca Galloway, see Tucker, *Tecumseh*, 77–80.

16 [John] Price-Brown, *Laura the undaunted* (Toronto: Ryerson 1930).

17 Michael Tait, 'Playwrights in a vacuum: English-Canadian drama in the nineteenth century,' *Canadian Literature* no. 16 (spring 1963): 9–10.

18 Biographical information on Mair comes from Shrive's definitive work; on the writing and completion of *Tecumseh* see 155, 177.

19 See Shrive, *Mair*, 61; Peter Charlebois, *The life of Louis Riel* (Toronto: NC Press

1975), 72–5; Mair, 'Memoirs and reminiscences,' *Tecumseh, a drama, and Canadian poems* (Toronto: Radisson Society 1926), xxxviii, xli, xlv.

20 Mair and Canada First: Shrive, *Mair*, 24–34, 52–82. See also his 'Canada First and Red River,' *Canadian Literature* no. 83 (winter 1979): 206–14.

21 Shrive, *Mair*, 152–5, 177.

22 John Matthews, 'Charles Mair,' in R.L. McDougall, ed., *Canada's past and present: a dialogue; our living tradition*, 5th ser. (Toronto: University of Toronto Press 1965), 83.

23 Mair, *Tecumseh*, act 1, scene 2; 5: 6.

24 Tait, 'Playwrights,' 12.

25 Shrive, *Mair*, 180,

26 Matthews, 'Mair,' 101.

27 Shrive, *Mair*, 182, 186.

28 Mair, *Tecumseh*, 253. *Tecumseh* never saw British publication, though Colonel Denison inveigled Matthew Arnold into giving sections of it a cursory, non-committal reading (Shrive, *Mair*, 169–70).

29 The gentle, social satire of *The imperialist* (1904) is not the stuff of tragedy but in a curious fashion Lorne becomes a kind of Tecumseh writ small. When in Mrs Duncan's Leacockian novel, Lorne Murchison travels to Britain in his quest for imperial federation, he finds there a hearty, business-as-usual indifference to the idealism that has sent him on his journey. Home again in Elgin, Ontario, he learns that the pragmatic boosters of material advancement have no time for his message either. Here are two very different writers displaying a common uneasiness about the imperial tie.

30 See Mair, *Dreamland* (ed. Shrive), xxxvi–xlii and 75–85, for original and revisions.

31 The Métis are, Mair wrote, 'a harmless obsequious set of men, and will, I believe, be very useful here when the country gets filled up' (*Globe* [Toronto], 14 Dec. 1868, 4). See also *Globe*, 16 Feb. 1869, 3. On the whipping, see Shrive, *Mair*, 73; the novel was Alexander Begg, '*Dot-it-down,' a story of life in the North-West* (Toronto: Hunter, Rose 1871).

32 *Globe* (Toronto), 28 May 1869, 3; 16 Feb. 1869, 3.

33 'The new Canada: its natural features and climate,' *Canadian Monthly and National Review* VIII (July and August 1875): 4, 164.

34 Mair, *Tecumseh*, 148–53; 'The American bison,' *Proceedings and Transactions of the Royal Society of Canada* 1st ser., VIII (1890): section II, 93.

35 Charles Mair, *Through the MacKenzie basin: a narrative of the Athabasca and Peace River treaty expedition of 1899* (Toronto: Wm. Briggs 1908), 6, 136.

36 Robert G. Haliburton, *The men of the north and their place in history* (Montreal: John Lovell 1869). See also Carl Berger, *Sense of power*, 128–33.

CHAPTER FIVE

1 Exceptions to the lack of critical attention exist, but it is noteworthy that
  Desmond Pacey's favourable (not especially laudatory, but not coldly dismissive
  either) comments appear in a four-page section of a chapter titled Fiction (1920–
  1940) in Carl F. Klinck. ed., *Literary history of Canada: Canadian literature in
  English* (2nd ed., 3 vols., Toronto: University of Toronto Press 1976), II,
  179–82, and in an introduction to the New Canadian Library edition of *Delight*
  (Toronto: McClelland and Stewart 1961). Ronald Hambleton's pioneering
  biography, *Mazo de la Roche of Jalna* (New York: Hawthorne 1966), remains a
  valuable work, but eschews any systematic critical approach. George Hendrick's monograph, *Mazo de la Roche* (New York: Twayne 1970), brings to its
  subject all the interest, admiration, and sympathy that Gibbon spent on his
  consideration of theologians. In view of de la Roche's prolific writing, it seems
  ironic that the best summation of her achievement occurs under her brief
  entry in Norah Story's *The Oxford companion to Canadian history and literature*
  (Toronto: Oxford University Press 1967), 206–7. See also Clara Thomas,
  'Mazo de la Roche,' in her *Our nature, our voices*, vol. 1 (Toronto: New Press
  1972), 101–3. Some of my conclusions parallel those of Jo-Ann Fellows, 'The
  "British Connection" in the Jalna novels of Mazo de la Roche: the Loyalist myth
  revisited,' *Dalhousie Review* 56 (summer 1976): 283–90. Unfortunately, I did
  not encounter this stimulating article until some time after this chapter had been
  completed. For sales figures, see Hambleton, *Mazo de la Roche*, 49–54.
2 Hendrick, title to chapter three, 59–98.
3 See de la Roche's letter to Mrs Kemp, 18 Apr. 1955, in the Mazo de la Roche
  collection (Fisher Rare Books Library, University of Toronto), box 6, and
  Dorothy Livesay, 'The making of Jalna,' *Canadian Literature* no. 23 (winter
  1965): 30; 'Exploring Jalna country', *Globe Magazine*, 3 Dec. 1966, 16.
4 Hambleton, *Mazo de la Roche*, 217.
5 Mazo de la Roche, *Explorers of the dawn*, foreword by Christopher Morley
  (New York: Grosset and Dunlap 1922), 12.
6 Mazo de la Roche, *Possession* (Toronto: Macmillan 1923).
7 Pacey, 'Fiction (1920–1940),' 669.
8 In view of the availability of Mazo de la Roche's Jalna series, textual citations
  will be followed by the abbreviated title and the number of the chapter from
  which the passage has been taken. The novels, their dates of publication, and
  their abbreviations are as follows:

Jalna (1927) J	*Young Renny* (1935) YR
Whiteoaks of Jalna (1929) WOJ	*Whiteoak harvest* (1936) HARVEST
Finch's fortune (1931) FF	*Whiteoak heritage* (1940) HERITAGE
The master of Jalna (1933) MOJ	*Wakefield's course* (1941) WC

The building of Jalna (1944) BOJ   *Whiteoak brothers* (1953) WB
Return to Jalna (1946) RTJ   *Variable winds at Jalna* (1954) VWJ
Mary Wakefield (1949) MW   *Centenary at Jalna* (1958) CJ
Renny's daughter (1951) RD   *Morning at Jalna* (1960) MJ

9 Mazo de la Roche, *Ringing the changes: an autobiography* (Toronto: Macmillan 1957), 2, 6, 9, 15.

10 See Robin Winks, *Canada and the United States: the Civil War years* (Baltimore: Johns Hopkins Press 1960), 237–43.

11 See also WOJ, 26; FF, 4; MW, 1; WB, 2.

12 The very important matter of money gives us a feel for the extent of the Jalna series' idealization of experience. Money is frequently mentioned in the cheerfully vulgar manner of the majority of the human race, but the means by which it is acquired remain generally romantic, at times fantastic. Large sums are acquired either through inheritance, horse races, or magical playwriting gifts. It would not suit their image for the Whiteoaks to be too skilled in financial matters, thus attempts to speculate result in catastrophe. The money's principal use is the upkeep of the property. Supposedly, the piggery and fruit farm, plus the racing stables, bring in adequate amounts of running money, but the reader is never vouchsafed many details about that. Over the century of its existence, approximately half of the original thousand acres has been sold to bail the Whiteoaks out of the financial mistakes to which they are prone.

The publisher Lovat Dickson's explanation of the series' British popularity also explains much else: 'The Whiteoak books represent the idealized picture of Canada which English people have' (Hambleton, *Mazo de la Roche*, 219).

13 See W.H. Graham, *The Tiger of Canada West* (Toronto: Clark, Irwin 1965).

14 We must realize that the inclusion of dates in the first novel indicates that a lengthy series had not initially been planned. Of course, the material flowed continuously and easily from her pencil. While she did write a number of other novels and miscellaneous works during her Jalna years, it was the series – as her publisher's letters and fan mail show – that sold. She became to an extent its willing prisoner. It was what the public wanted. It maintained her expensive living habits. Her fiction may reveal a perpetually girlish sensibility, but her extensive financial correspondence presents a capable businesswoman in close touch with the marketplace.

15 Quoted in Edward Weeks to M. de la Roche, 4 Feb. 1933, De la Roche collection, box 9.

16 Edward Weeks, *In friendly candor* (Boston: Little, Brown 1959), 89.

17 No reader can ignore in this context the sheer vaudeville fun of Wakefield Whiteoak, supposedly bound for the monastery following his conversion to Romanism, stripping off his cassock at a family dinner to reveal to his brothers a dinner-jacket beneath, signifying his return to the secular world (HARVEST, 31).

18 De la Roche, *Ringing the changes*, 200.
19 Lest the reader bridle at the use of a plant with American nomenclature for symbolic purposes at Jalna, recall that the Old Dominion has its charms for the Whiteoaks, who note that a woman comes from ' "a good Virginian family. Her people used to keep slaves" ' (FF, 6).
20 Mazo de la Roche, *Quebec: historic seaport* (Garden city: Doubleday, Doran 1944). One of the Jalna characters, when visiting the Citadel of Quebec, reads from her copy of *The golden dog* (HERITAGE, 10).
21 Ronald Hambleton, *The secret of Jalna* (Toronto: General Publishing 1972), 163–72. The portrait of the novelist here seems far less restrained than in Hambleton's biography of her.

CHAPTER SIX

1 See Sacvan Bercovitch, 'How the Puritans won the American Revolution,' *Massachesetts Review* 17 (winter 1976): 597–630.
2 Parts of this chapter appeared in a different form in my 'Upper Canadian Loyalism: what the textbooks tell,' *Journal of Canadian Studies* 12 (spring 1977): 17–26. Other summaries of the Loyalist myth occur in Jo-Ann Fellows, 'The Loyalist myth in Canada,' Canadian Historical Association, *Historical papers, 1971*, 96–106, and Murray W. Barkley, 'The Loyalist tradition in New Brunswick,' *Acadiensis* IV (spring, 1975): 3–7.
3 A stimulating account of this and related cultural matters, to which I am indebted, may be found in William DeVilliers Westfall, 'The dominion of the Lord: an introduction to the cultural history of Protestant Ontario,' *Queen's Quarterly* 83 (spring 1976): 47–70.
4 See Winthrop Sargent, ed., *The Loyalist poetry of the Revolution* (Philadelphia 1857), 1–24, 56–7, 117–18, 129–31. For the rebel counterblast: Frank Moore, ed., *Songs and ballads of the American Revolution* (New York: D. Appleton 1856). For songs of both sides: Oscar Brand, ed., *Songs of '76: a folksinger's history of the Revolution* (New York: M. Evans 1972).
5 'Stanzas. Written on the 10th of May, 1776, by an exile from America.' The poem, found in Sargent, ed., *Loyalist poetry*, 89–90, is the work of one of the most intellectually distinguished of the Loyalists, the Reverend Dr Myles Cooper, president of King's College (now Columbia University), tutor of Washington's stepson.
6 J.J. Talman, ed., *Loyalist narratives from Upper Canada* (Toronto: Champlain Society 1946), 75–6.
7 Robert Sellar, a turn-of-the-century historical novelist who deals with Upper Canadian Loyalism, uses the figure of Moses to describe Loyalist leaders in *Morven* (1911) and *Hemlock* (1890).

8 Talman, ed., *Loyalist narratives*, 72.
9 'The adherents to the royal cause felt that loyalty to the sovereign was their first and highest duty – that it was enjoined upon them by all the influences and associations of natural tradition, early teaching, and natural instinct, as well as by the divine authority of God himself,' J. George Hodgins, *A history of Canada and of the other British provinces in North America* (Montreal: John Lovell 1866), 145.
10 William F. Coffin, *1812: the war, and its moral* (Montreal: John Lovell 1864), 40–1.
11 William H. Withrow, *A history of Canada* (Toronto: Copp Clark 1876), 114.
12 Charles R. Tuttle, *An illustrated history of the dominion*, vol. 1 (Montreal: Downie 1877), 320.
13 W.H.P. Clement, *History of the dominion of Canada* (Toronto: Wm. Briggs 1897), 127. C.G.D. Roberts, *A history of Canada* (1897; Toronto: Morang 1902), 202.
14 An undated notice from the *Montreal Gazette* concerning Robert Sellar's *Hemlock* (1890) is reprinted on the end papers of *Morven* (1911). The hands invoked by Sir Charles G.D. Roberts in 1897 are not engaged in hewing a national destiny but in the newspaper notice they retain sufficient concreteness to have been developing Canada from 'the wilderness that it was to the fertile and cultivated garden that it is today.' However symbolic the concept as expressed here, real hands can cultivate real gardens. Roberts, however, in his textbooks displays an idealism and vagueness that exists in his serious work as well. For example, the wide gap between Sir Charles Roberts' poems employing real or ideal subjects can be gauged by contrasting 'The Potato Harvest' with 'Origins.' It is only in his finest works such as 'The Tantramar Revisited' that a bleak Wordsworthianism enables him to reconcile what are almost two universes.
15 Considerable help in locating historical fiction on the Loyalists came from Murray Barkley, 'Selected sample list of novels, epic poems, and children's fiction on the Loyalists and the war of 1812,' *Loyalist Gazette* xv (spring 1976): 14.
16 See Frank Baird's *Roger Davis, Loyalist* (1907), H.A. Cody's *The king's arrow* (1927), and John F. Hayes' *On Loyalist trails* (1971). Flight, escape, and the overcoming of figures who stand in the way of safety seems a perennial theme of children's fiction. So also does the theme of proving oneself a match for a new environment. The Loyalist experience presents such material readily to the hands of writers, giving a public resonance to their characters' crises and achievements, which accounts for the use of Loyalism in adventure fiction over a long period.
17 C. Holmes MacGillivray, *The shadow of tradition: a tale of old Glengarry* (Ottawa: Graphic 1927), preface.

18 Allan Smith, 'American culture and the English Canadian mind at the end of the nineteenth century,' *Journal of Popular Culture* IV (spring 1971): 1045–51.

19 Ralph Connor [Charles William Gordon], *The runner* (Toronto: Doubleday, Doran and Gundy 1929), 262.

20 Maida Parlow French, *All this to keep* (Toronto: Collins 1947), 214, 220–5.

21 French, *Boughs bend over* (Toronto: McClelland and Stewart 1943), 54–5, 200–1. For Denison, see his 'The United Empire Loyalists' in J. Castell Hopkins, ed., *Canada: an encyclopedia of the country*, vol. 1 (Toronto 1898), 109.

22 Contrast W.S. Wallace's *History of the Canadian people* (Toronto: Copp Clark 1930), which terms the Loyalist migration 'one of the most touching episodes of modern history' (134). This, after Armenia and the Somme! See also his *First book of Canadian history* (Toronto: Macmillan 1928), which sniffs that the Loyalists were 'subject to persecution of a most unchristian character' (86).

23 John L. Field and Lloyd Dennis, *Land of promise* (Toronto: House of Grant 1960), 318.

24 See, for example, [Michael Gonder Scherck], *Pen pictures of early pioneer life in Upper Canada* (Toronto: Wm Briggs 1905); W.S. Herrington, *Pioneer life among the Loyalists in Upper Canada* (Toronto: Macmillan 1915); Edwin C. Guillet, *Early life in Upper Canada* ([Toronto]: Ontario Publishing Co. 1933).

25 Carl Berger, *The writing of Canadian history* (Toronto: Oxford University Press 1976), 137–59.

26 See, for example, an article in the official publication of the Ontario Human Rights Commission: 'For these Loyalists who eventually formed the core of the colony's ruling oligarchies, and whose descendants still claim a special, almost aristocratic social precedence, Canada was a land of second choice.' Harold Troper, 'Immigration: an historical perspective,' *Human Relations* 16 (1976–7): 7.

27 Zena Cherry, 'Column,' *Globe and Mail* (Toronto, 2 Jan. 1976), 11; Peter C. Newman, *The Canadian establishment*, vol. 1 (Toronto: McClelland and Stewart 1975), 376.

CHAPTER SEVEN

1 *Report of the Royal Commission on National Development in the Arts, Letters, and Sciences* (Massey Report) (Ottawa 1951), 4. My thanks to Professor William Westfall for calling this to my attention.

2 R.D. MacDonald, 'The persuasiveness of Grant's *Lament for a nation,*' *Studies in Canadian Literature* 2 (summer 1977): 245–6. For an equally perceptive commentary that appeared too late for discussion here, see Eli Mandel, 'George

Grant: language, nation, the silence of God,' *Canadian Literature* no. 83 (winter 1979), 163–75

3 John Muggeridge, 'George Grant's anguished conservatism,' in Larry Schmidt, ed., *George Grant in process; essays and conversations* (hereafter *GGP*) (Toronto: Anansi 1978), 40–8. A more telling use of Loyalism in explaining Grant occurs in Ramsay Cook, 'Loyalism, technology, and Canada's fate,' in *The maple leaf forever* (Toronto: Macmillan 1971), 51–4.

4 See George Grant, 'A platitude,' in *Technology and empire* (hereafter *TE*) (Toronto: Anansi 1969), 140. The imputation of ancestral determinism at which Grant takes umbrage may be found in Robert Blumstock, 'Anglo-Saxon lament,' *Canadian Review of Sociology and Anthropology* 3 (1966): 104, and in R.K. Crook, 'Modernization and nostalgia: a note on the sociology of pessimism,' *Queen's Quarterly* 73 (summer 1966): 284.

5 George Grant. 'Conversation: intellectual background,' *GGP*, 63.

6 George Grant, 'Revolution and tradition,' in Lionel Rubinoff, ed., *Tradition and revolution* (Toronto: Macmillan 1971), 89.

7 Grant, 'In defence of North America,' *TE*, 24–5.

8 George Grant, 'An ethic of community,' in M. Oliver, ed., *Social purpose for Canada* (Toronto: University of Toronto Press 1961), 26.

9 George Grant, 'Preface,' to Scott Symons, *Heritage: a romantic look at early Canadian furniture* (Toronto: McClelland and Stewart 1971).

10 George Grant, *Lament for a nation* (Toronto: McClelland and Stewart 1965), 3.

11 George Grant, 'Have we a Canadian nation?' *Public Affairs* VIII (1945): 165.

12 Very briefly, John Ruskin interpreted the Renaissance as an exaltation of the technically skilled but showily monumental spirit in art and architecture. Slickness of execution masked the dehumanized nature of the new work. T.S. Eliot saw cultural fall in terms of a 'dissociation of sensibility,' a process in which thought and feeling grew divorced and their expression diverse and constricted. In our own time, Marshall McLuhan's communication theories have rested on a similar vision of dissociation, in which auditory and visual modes of expression reduced themselves and our culture to impoverished overdependence upon univocal modes of discourse. Key passages for these authors are as follows: for Ruskin, see *The stones of Venice* (1851–3), especially its section on 'The nature of Gothic'; for Eliot, see 'The metaphysical poets' (1921); for McLuhan, see *The Gutenberg galaxy* (1962). See also Dennis Duffy, *Marshall McLuhan* (Toronto: McClelland and Stewart 1969), 26–31.

13 George Grant, 'Plato and Popper,' *Canadian Journal of Economics and Political Science* XX (1954): 187.

14 The inability of the British conservative tradition behind Loyalism to withstand the onslaught of modernity is mentioned by Grant again in 'Canadian fate and

imperialism,' *TE*, 68, and in the introduction to the Carleton Library edition of *Lament* (Toronto: McClelland and Stewart 1970), x–xi.

15 George Grant, *Time as history* (Toronto: CBC Publications 1969), 29–30; see also 'The university curriculum,' *TE*, 116.

16 George Grant, 'Value and technology,' Canadian Conference on Social Welfare, *Proceedings*, 1964, 23. On his personal beliefs, he has written: 'I believed in a moral order which men did not measure and define but by which we were measured and defined,' *Philosophy in the mass age* (2nd ed., Toronto: Copp Clark 1966), v.

17 Grant, *Philosophy in the mass age*, 7.

18 See, for example, the opening pages of Grant's *Time as history* and 'Revolution and tradition' in Rubinoff, ed., *Tradition and revolution*; also 'Knowing and meaning,' *Transactions of the Royal Society of Canada*, 4th ser., XII (1974): 61.

19 Grant, 'In defence of North America,' *TE*, 34. See as well, Grant, 'Canadian fate and imperialism,' *TE*, 74; *Philosophy in the mass age* (1966), vi; 'The computer does not impose on us the ways it should be used,' in A. Rotstein, ed., *Beyond industrial growth* (Toronto: University of Toronto Press 1976), 118–19.

20 Grant, 'In defence of North America,' *TE*, 37; 'Canadian fate and imperialism,' *TE*, 77.

21 Grant, *Philosophy in the mass age* (1966), vii–viii.

22 Grant, *Lament*, 97.

23 Grant, 'Revolution and tradition,' 85.

24 Lee has noted that 'it was when I began to read a series of essays by the philosopher George Grant that I started to comprehend what we had been living inside.' See 'Cadence, country, silence,' *Open Letter*, ser. 2, no. 6 (fall 1973): 42. The entire article has much to relate about Grant's effect on Lee and others. In view of these ties, it is interesting to observe that *A new Athens*, with its evocation of Loyalist vestiges, has for its jacket design a detail from C.W. Jefferys' drawing of a rail fence. The drawing first appeared in a work by Scott Symons' father. See H.L. Symons, *Fences* (Toronto: Ryerson 1958).

25 George Grant, 'The university curriculum,' *TE*, 132.

26 Scott Symons, 'Interview,' in Graeme Gibson, ed., *Eleven Canadian novelists* (Toronto: Anansi 1975), 324.

27 Scott Symons, 'Rosedale ain't what it used to be,' *Toronto Life*, October 1972, 42.

28 Scott Symons, *Heritage*. Since the work is unpaginated but organized into sections around the photographs of single pieces of furniture, my references will be made to the number and title of the relevant section (in this case section 5, Tulles grandfather clock).

29 Symons, *Heritage*, section 29, Rustic Queen Anne table.

30 Symons, 'Rosedale ain't what it used to be,' 54.

31 Manuscript of second draft of Symons, *Canada: duel or dialogue* (unpub., Sept. 1962), 307, located in Scott Symons papers, Trinity College Library, Toronto.

32 Symons, 'The meaning of English Canada,' *Continuous Learning* II (Nov.–Dec. 1963), 254; *Place d'Armes, a personal narrative* (Toronto: McClelland and Stewart 1967), 60, 178; *Civic square: an original manuscript* (Toronto: McClelland and Stewart 1969), 86, 209.

33 Symons, *Civic square*, 179–80. Symons' foes are further explored in Charles Taylor's chapter on him in *Six journeys: a Canadian pattern* (Toronto: Anansi 1977), 207.

34 Symons, *Heritage*, section 7, Marble mantlepiece.

35 Symons, 'From *Helmet of flesh*,' *Canadian Fiction Magazine*, no. 24 / 25 (spring / summer 1977): 89–102.

36 I am grateful for Professor Clara Thomas' independent confirmation of this judgment I had then recently made. Letter to author, 25 Oct. 1978.

37 Symons, 'Rosedale ain't what it used to be,' 55. Emphasis in the original.

38 Symons, *Civic square*, 5.

39 Robert Fulford's unsympathetic review – 'A monster from Toronto,' *Toronto Star*, 26 Jan. 1967, 23 – contains a just appraisal of Symons' strengths and weaknesses as a writer despite its lurid title. 'When *Place d'Armes* is interesting it is neither good nor bad literature, it is a kind of higher journalism, an artistically arranged set of facts and opinions.'

40 Dennis Lee, *The gods* (Toronto: McClelland and Stewart 1979), 17. (Reprinted by permission of McClelland and Stewart Limited, Toronto.)

41 Lee, 'Cadence, country, silence,' 47. My analysis of Lee's writing has benefitted greatly from his comments on an earlier version of this text. Indeed, many of my comments are no more than clumsy paraphrases of the poet's.

42 See the title sequence from *Kingdom of absence* (Toronto: Ananse [sic] 1967), 31–8.

43 Dennis Lee, *Civil elegies and other poems* (Toronto: Anansi 1972). Reference to the title sequence will consist of indicating the number of the poem in the sequence and the page on which the cited text appears, as in the present: 1, 34, 33. (Reprinted by permission of Anansi Publishers, Toronto.)

44 Geoffrey Scott, *The architecture of humanism* (2nd ed., London: Constable 1924), 143–5.

45 Dennis Lee, *Savage fields: an essay in literature and cosmology* (Toronto: Anansi 1977), 3.

46 George Grant, 'A platitude,' *TE*, 143.

47 Al Purdy, 'I Think It Was Wednesday,' *The Cariboo horses* (Toronto: McClelland and Stewart 1965), 98–100. All quotations from Purdy are reprinted by permission of McClelland and Stewart Limited, Toronto.

48 Gary Geddes, 'A.W. Purdy: an interview,' *Canadian Literature* no. 41 (summer 1969): 66.

49 Al Purdy, *Being alive: poems, 1958–78* (Toronto: McClelland and Stewart 1978).

50 Geddes, 'A.W. Purdy,' 69–70. The poem, 'Roblin Mills' (later 'Roblin's Mills (2)'), appeared in *Tamarack Review* 33 (autumn 1964): 11.

51 E.W. Mandel, 'Turning new leaves (1),' *Canadian Forum* XLII (March 1963): 280.

52 This quotation from *In search of Owen Roblin* (Toronto: McClelland and Stewart 1974) is found on the final page; further references to this unpaginated work will be according to my own count from the title-page. 'Roblin's Mills (2)' can also be found in *Being alive*, 56–7.

53 See Purdy, 'Elegy for a Grandfather' in *Emu, remember!* (Fredericton: Fiddlehead 1968), 2. The final version is cited here, and appears in *Being alive*, 54–5.

54 Both available in *Being alive*, 50–1 and 91. That same volume contains three poems later cited: 'My Grandfather's Country,' 125–7; 'Wilderness Gothic,' 81, and 'The Country North of Belleville,' 22–3.

55 Purdy, 'Bon Jour,' in his *No other country* (Toronto: McClelland and Stewart 1977), 136.

Index

Except for entries of particular importance, no single-mention items are listed.

This book was designed by WILLIAM ROSS

and printed at the UNIVERSITY OF TORONTO PRESS.